WITH LOVE, LITHUANIA

With love
LITHUANIA

NACIONALINĖ
KNYGA

ISBN 9955-495-15-4

UDK 914(474.5)(084)

Vi328

Compiled by

Virgilijus Butkevičius

Jonas Dovydėnas

Diana Januševičiūtė

Coauthors

Aldona Mikulionienė

Alma Kusaitė

Audronė Galvonaitė

Auksė Livija Kasperaitienė

Birutė Imbrasienė

Daiva Vikmonienė

Gražina Jurgaitienė

Indrė Daunytė

Laimonas Gryva

Olga Babošina

Ramūnas Terleckas

Selemonas Paltanavičius

Skaidrė Vainikauskaitė

Viktorija Mitkutė

Marius Laurinavičius

Designed by

Gediminas Trečiokas

Translated by

Vytautas Petrukaitis

Translation edited by

Aušrinė Byla, M. A.

Publisher

UAB „Nacionalinė knyga"

Kareivių St 6, Vilnius, Lithuania

Phone +370 5 277 76 96

www.nknyga.lt

Printed by

AB „Spauda"

Printed on paper *Luxo Satin* 170 gsm

manufactured by 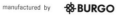 **BURGO**

supplied by

The photographs in this publication are by

Albinas Slavinskas

Algimantas Aleksandravičius

Antanas Lukšėnas

Antanas Varanka

Artūras Užgailis

Dmitrij Matvejev

Gediminas Trečiokas

Gintaras Karosas

Jonas Kliučius

Klaudijus Driskius

Leonas Jonys

Mykolas Okulič-Kazarinas

Mindaugas Kulbis (*Lietuvos rytas*)

Ramūnas Virkutis

Robertas Kananavičius

Romualdas Požerskis

Selemonas Paltanavičius

Tomas Vyšniauskas

Vytas Karaciejus

Vytautas Knyva

Vytautas Šerėnas

Zenonas Nekrošius

Tomas Reventas

Jonas Staselis (*Lietuvos rytas*)

Other photographs are by photographers from the ELTA Agency: Gediminas Žilinskas, Kęstutis Vanagas, Tomas Bauras....

Also from the archive of the Presidency of the Republic of Lithuania (photographer Džoja Gunda Barysaitė)

From the archive of AB Lietuvos energija (photographer Petras Apanavičius and a photograph of RIC Agency)

From the archive of ISM (photographer Tomas Lopata)

From the archive of the Ballooning Center

From the archive of FORUM PALACE (photographers Mikhail Levin and Mindaugas Kulbis)

From the archive of Žalgiris Kaunas Basketball Club

From the archive of Lithuanian Football Federation (photos by INNA Agency)

The slides of the pictures *The Fairy Tale of the Kings* and *The Castle Fairy Tale* by M. K. Čiurlionis are from the funds of the M. K. Čiurlionis National Art Museum (photographer Arūnas Baltėnas)

Photographs of Vytautas the Great War Museum

Photographs of the Lithuanian Archive of Image and Sound

Photographs of the Ministry of Defense of the Republic of Lithuania

Also used is the illustration of the 1613 map by Mikalojaus Kristupas Radvila from the publication *The Old Maps of Lithuania*

The compilers wish to acknowledge the assistance of the
following people and organizations in preparing the book:

The President's Office of the Republic of Lithuania (Dalia Kutraitė-Giedraitienė)

The Seimas of the Republic of Lithuania (Andrius Vaišnys)

The Ministry of Defense of the Republic of Lithuania

  (Marius Alekna, Tomas Urbonas)

The Ministry of Culture of the Republic of Lithuania (Indrė Daunytė)

The Ministry of Transport and Communications of the Republic of Lithuania

  (Inona Brasiūnienė)

The Ministry of Education and Culture of the Republic of Lithuania (Nomeda Barauskienė)

The Ministry of Economy of the Republic of Lithuania (Ričardas Slapšys)

The Ministry of Foreign Affairs of the Republic of Lithuania (Ramūnas Misiulis)

Lithuanian Development Agency (Ernesta Dapkienė)

The Municipality of Kaunas City

The Information Society Development Committee under the Government

  of the Republic of Lithuania (Linas Pečiūra)

The Martynas Mažvydas Lithuanian National Library (Vytautas Gudaitis)

The Lithuanian Art Museum (Vytautas Balčiūnas)

The M. K. Čiurlionis National Art Museum

Vytautas the Great War Museum

Lithuanian Folk Culture Center (Juozas Mikutavičius)

Institute for Design and Restoration (Rimas Grigas)

Lithuanian Confederation of Industrialists (Dmitrijus Slepniovas)

Lietuvos rytas daily (Marius Laurinavičius)

Verslo žinios daily (Aušra Barysienė, Ramūnas Terleckas)

Aviacijos pasaulis newspaper (Vilma Jankienė, Gintarė Rimkuvienė)

Europos parkas Non-profit Public Institution (Gintaras Karosas)

Oreivystės centras Public Institution

  (Jolanta Tūraitė-Koncevičienė, Romualdas Bakanauskas)

Klaipėda's State Seaport Authority

UAB „Blikas" (Gytis Lagunavičius)

Cafe „Nendrinė pastogė"

Elnias Golf Club

We would like to thank the participants of the publication
With Love, Lithuania

State

Lithuania is an independent democratic republic. Its governing institutions are the Seimas, the president, and the government. The president is elected by popular vote for a five-year term. The legislative body is the Seimas (parliament) consisting of 141 members, each elected by voters' ballots for a four-year term. The government with the prime minister in charge is answerable to the Seimas. The powers of the authorities are restricted by the Constitution.

Coat of arms

The coat of arms of Lithuania is the *Vytis*. It is a knight in armor riding a horse and holding a sword in one hand, and a shield in the other. The field of the shield is blue inlaid with a double cross. The knight and horse are silver.

National anthem

Tautiška giesmė (National Song) by V. Kudirka is the Lithuanian national anthem. The patriotic poem became the national anthem in 1919, after V. Kudirka's death.

Flag

The Lithuanian flag is tricolor, made up of yellow, green and red stripes of the same width. These are the colors prevailing in Lithuanian folk textiles. The yellow of the flag symbolizes the fertile fields of Lithuania, gold with ripe grain. The green symbolizes the vitality of the nature and the people. The red is the symbol of blood shed when fighting for the freedom of the homeland.

Capital

Vilnius is the capital of the Republic of Lithuania. Its name was first mentioned in written sources in 1323. In 1994, the Old Town of Vilnius was included in UNESCO's list of World Heritage Sites. The population of Vilnius according to the data of 2001 was approximately 600,000.

Currency

The Lithuanian national currency *litas* was introduced in 1922. After the country regained independence, *litas* was reintroduced on June 25, 1993. The name *litas* is derived from the first three letters of the Latin name for Lithuania (*Lituania*). One hundredth of a *litas* is called a cent. At present the *litas* is pegged to the €. The official exchange rate is 3.4528 LT to 1 €.

Population

According to the 2001 census, the country's population is approximately 3.5 million, four fifths of whom are Lithuanian. Nearly 70 percent live in towns, the rest in rural areas.

The average population density is 57 people per square kilometer. In comparison with other European countries it is relatively low. Vilnius and Kaunas Counties with 87 residents per square kilometer on the average are the most densely populated, and Utena County with 26 residents is the sparsest.

The average life expectancy of the Lithuanian population has been increasing. Now it is 67 years for men and about 77.5 years for women.

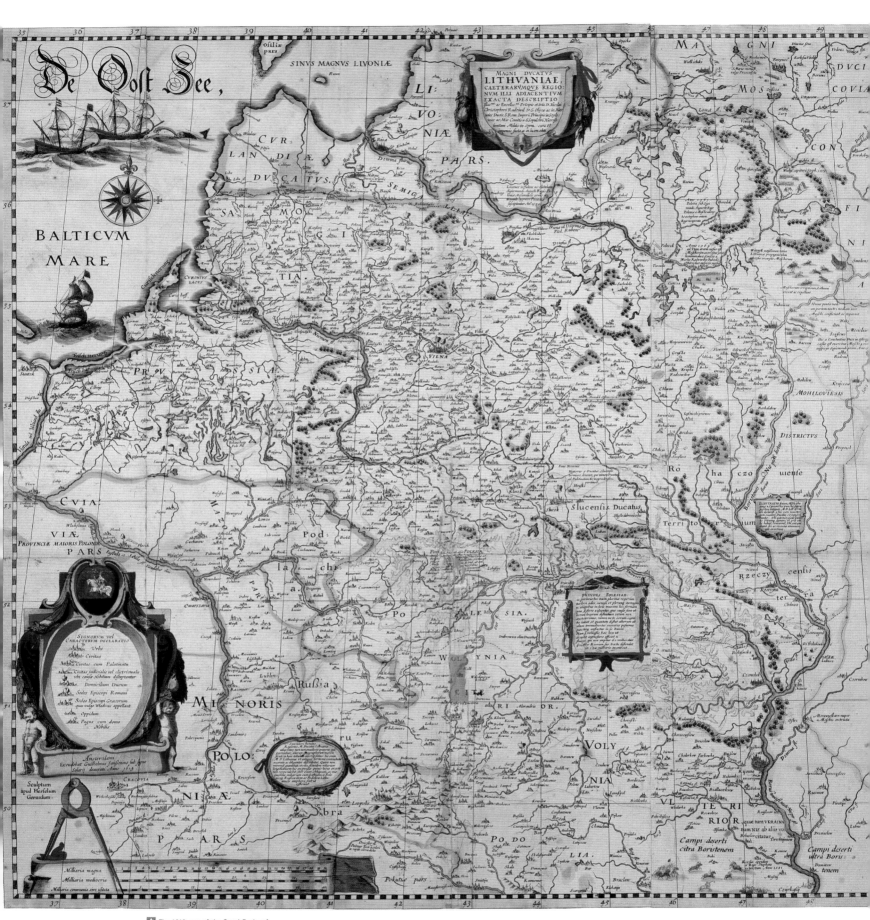

The 1613 map of the Grand Duchy of Lithuania by Mikalojus Kristupas Radvila is regarded as a masterpiece of baroque cartography. The original map is now in the Library of Vilnius University.

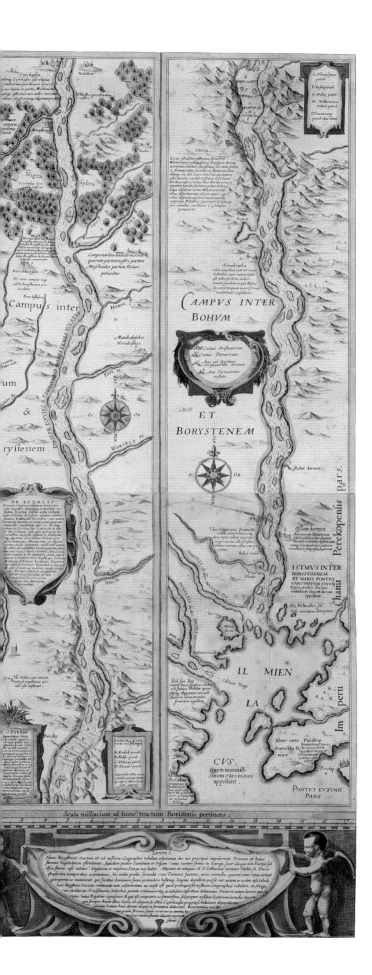

Land

Lithuania looks like a tiny dot on the map of the world. Actually the country occupying 65.3 thousand square kilometers is one and a half times larger than Denmark or the Netherlands, and twice as large as Belgium.

The sandy western coast of Lithuania is washed by the cool waves of the Baltic Sea. In the north, east, and west it borders with the neighboring countries of Latvia, Belarus, Poland, and the Kaliningrad Region of the Russian Federation. The geographical center of Europe is in Lithuania, in Vilnius County.

Hilly highlands of Lithuania give way to flat lowlands. A third of the country's territory is covered with dense deciduous and coniferous forests, meadows taking up another fifth.

Switzerland and Austria are sometimes called countries of lakes scattered among mountains. Lithuania might be referred to as a country of lakes scattered among hills. Over three thousand lakes of different sizes dapple the Lithuanian landscape. They are located mostly in the east and southeast. This is an area, one of the most abundant in lakes in Europe, formed after the last glacier receded. Drūkšiai, Lithuania's largest lake with an area of over 42 square kilometers, also lies there.

Almost one thousand rivers and streams crisscross the country. The longest is the Nemunas. Its overall length is 937 kilometers, of which 475 km. are in Lithuanian territory. Its source is in Belarus and it flows across Lithuania before spilling into the Baltic Sea. The Neris, Lithuania's second largest river, flows into the Nemunas in Kaunas.

The country's climate is similar to that of Poland, except for the coastal area, which resembles that of Western Europe. The average annual air temperature in Lithuania is 6^0 C. The mean air temperature in winter is -4.9^0 C, and 17.0^0 C in summer.

The average annual precipitation is 748 mm. In fall and winter, southwestern and southern winds prevail. In spring, more often than not, they blow from the northwest, and in summer from the west. In inland areas, the average wind velocity is 3-3.5 m/s, and on the coast as high as 5.5-6 m/s.

Language

The Lithuanian language belongs to the Baltic group of Indo-European languages. Latvian and Lithuanian are the only languages of the group that are still spoken today. The sonorous and rich Lithuanian language is particularly valuable from a scientific viewpoint, as it has preserved numerous features characteristic of the ancient parent language. In the early 20th century, modern Lithuanian was standardized by the linguist Jonas Jablonskis (1861-1930). Standard Lithuanian is based on the melodious dialect of western *Aukštaičiai* (*Suvalkiečiai*). In 1918, Lithuanian was proclaimed the state language, however, it lost that status during the Soviet times. It became the state language again in 1988. Now its is used as the means of communication in all government and public institutions of the Republic of Lithuania.

From the Baltic to the Black sea

Lithuania's history of statehood begins in the 13th century, when Mindaugas (? – 1263), having united the feuding dukes by force and ingenuity, came to the throne. Thus the foundation was laid for the Grand Duchy of Lithuania (GDL), one of the most powerful and influential states of medieval Europe. Mindaugas strove for international recognition of the Lithuanian state and that was why in 1251 he accepted baptism. Two years later, he was crowned and became the first and only King of Lithuania. After Mindaugas was killed, Lithuania reverted to paganism once again.

Several decades after Mindaugas's death, the dynasty of Gediminas came to power. Now the country became stronger and more modernized. Its borders expanded from the Baltic to the Black Sea. The nobility formed, which became the staunchest supporters of grand dukes. Although Grand Duke Gediminas (r. 1316-1341) was not the originator of the dynasty, its name is associated with this gifted ruler and diplomat.

It is known from the letters Gediminas wrote to the Pope that the pagan sovereign also intended to accept baptism. The Grand Duke tried to convince the Holy Father that he was fighting to defend his country against crusaders and not because he wanted to destroy the Christian faith.

Soon after Gediminas's death, Algirdas (r. 1345-1377) took over the helm of the country. His brother, Kęstutis, helped him to rule. Algirdas strengthened the influence of the GDL in the East. Thanks to him, large areas of Slavic lands came under the rule of the Grand Duchy, and the disastrous onslaught of Mongols and Tartars to the West was stopped. The strong Lithuanian state of that time protected the rest of Europe from devastating wars with hordes of Tartars.

While Algirdas was busy on the eastern fringes of the GDL, his brother Kęstutis defended the western borders from crusaders with a sword and through negotiations. Legend has it that Kęstutis met the priestess Birutė in Palanga. The two were so smitten with love that the girl forsook her duties to pagan gods and together with Kęstutis eloped to Trakai, the old capital of Lithuania. Their eldest son, Vytautas, was born there.

The sovereign Vytautas the Great (r. 1392-1430) is the most prominent figure in the history of Lithuania. While continuing the policy of his predecessors, Vytautas went on strengthening the state from the inside and sent obedient deputies to the lands of the GDL that were now scattered over vast expanses. Having formed a commonwealth with the Kingdom of Poland after the Krėva Agreement of 1385, the Grand Duchy of Lithuania accepted Christianity two years later. This step brought about sudden changes within the society and the state. Towns were granted the Magdeburg Rights, the nobility was legitimized, large land ownership and written culture took root replacing the standards of common law that had prevailed in Lithuania prior to Christianity.

However, the union with Poland and the christening did not put an end to the crusaders' onslaughts and did not help to solve the conflicts regarding the western borders of the Grand Duchy. Tension grew between German knights and Lithuanians. Diplomatic means were exhausted, and weapons were raised once more to settle disagreements.

In 1410, together with his cousin Jogaila, the Grand Duke of Lithuania and the King of Poland, and a joint army,

Vytautas the Great sapped the vital powers of the Order of the Knights of the Cross. Having suffered a crushing defeat, the Order grew weak and soon ceased to exist. The schemes of German knights to get firmly established in the Lithuanian lands fell through forever. The power of the Grand Duchy reached its peak. However, from the end of the 15th century, united Russia became a major threat to Lithuania. Trying to fend off Russia's influence, Lithuania turned to Poland for support.

As a result of the Lublin Agreement of 1569, the Grand Duchy was even more tightly intertwined with the Kingdom of Poland. The joint Polish-Lithuanian monarchy was formed whose territories and military potential were comparable with the kingdoms of Great Britain or Spain of the time.

The golden age of the Lithuanian and Polish monarchies lasted about a hundred years. Internal conflicts and the assaults of enemy troops accelerated its decline. Two hundred-odd years later, in 1759, the Lithuanian-Polish Commonwealth was finally divided among three influential empires of the time: Russia, Austria, and Prussia. The territory of present-day Lithuania came under the rule of tsarist Russia and for more than two centuries it disappeared from the political map of the world.

The 19th century was an especially difficult and painful time for Lithuania. After the suppressed rebellion of 1863, the tsar intensified russification in Lithuania. His decree of 1864 banned Lithuanian publications in Latin characters. The public in Western Europe realized the threats facing Lithuanians – that of losing their native tongue, and that of Catholicism being replaced by Russian Orthodoxy. The tsar's policy encountered enormous resistance by the public in Lithuania. Books in Latin characters were printed in the neighboring countries where the tsar's decree was not valid. Until the ban was lifted in 1904, prohibited publications were secretly bootlegged into Lithuania by the so-called book-smugglers.

The first period of independence

At the beginning of the 20th century, revolutions jolted Russia one after another. World War I further weakened the tsarist land that was nicknamed 'the jail of nations'. The exhausted empire began to ignore the events occurring in its far-away provinces, and a favorable opportunity sprang up for Lithuania to declare independence.

A group of intelligentsia made use of this favorable political situation to announce the Declaration of Independence on February 16, 1918. The period of establishing a free state was set in motion. Agriculture grew stronger, industries developed, armed forces were being created, and the foundation for a modern culture was being laid.

The situation in the newly independent state was similar to that of many other countries of Central Europe. After a brief period of prospering democracy, in 1926, A. Smetona took power and introduced authoritarian rule. This, however, did not hinder the fast growth of the economy and the wellbeing of the population.

Lithuania was free for only two decades. In late 1939, the USSR and Germany, apprehensive of impending war, struck a secret treaty that divided Europe into zones controlled by their influence. In accordance with the Molotov-Ribbentrop Pact of August 23, 1939, Lithuania was handed over to Germany. On September 28 of the same year, the former agreement was modified, and Germany gave the country to the Soviet Union.

The paper agreements were soon implemented. In 1940, at the beginning of World War II, the Soviet Union occupied Lithuania. By Stalin's order, tens of thousands of Lithuanians, who could at least allegedly harm Soviet authority, were exiled to Siberia. Only a tiny part of Lithuania's elite managed to escape to the West. When Nazi Germany declared war against the USSR on June 22, 1941, Lithuania was occupied by new invaders. This period in the history of Lithuania was fraught with atrocities, one of which was the tragedy of the Holocaust.

Rebirth

In the 1980s, the President of the USSR Mikhail Gorbachev declared *perestroika*. It was expected to revitalize the stagnant political and economic life of the Soviet Union and to ameliorate the totalitarian regime. The KGB's influence grew weaker, and the Iron Curtain separating the USSR from the West started to crumble. *Perestroika* intensified the will to regain statehood in the Baltic countries, Lithuania, Latvia, and Estonia. *Sajūdis* (the Movement for Perestroika), established in 1988, started openly declaring the idea of a free Lithuania. In August 1989, the three Baltic states commemorated the fiftieth anniversary of the Molotov-Ribbentrop Pact. Millions of peaceful people came to the event called the Baltic Road. They linked hands and made a live chain from the tower of Gediminas Castle and Vilnius Cathedral to Tompea Castle Tower in Tallinn. This was their way of expressing their determination to jointly seek freedom.

On March 11, 1990, the Supreme Council of Lithuania, the Reconstituent *Seimas*, restored the independent Republic of Lithuania. Latvia and Estonia soon followed suit. The USSR, indignant at this step, made Lithuania suspend the Act of Independence and declared an economic blockade. The situation of the new state became ambiguous: it did not renounce its independence, however, there was no way to utilize it.

In January 1991, the USSR decided to use force on the Lithuania that had not renounced its sovereignty. The Soviet army started seizing one strategic target after another – the Press House, the railway station. They did not allow planes to land. On the night of January 13th, tanks surrounded the television tower in Vilnius. On that night, fourteen people were killed under the tracks of tanks and armored cars, and thousands were injured.

After seizing control over radio and television, the Soviet troops started approaching the *Seimas* Palace where parliament was in session. Here the troops were confronted by nearly twenty thousand people who had come from all over Lithuania. The military did not dare attack them.

The entire world learned about the atrocities of the USSR's soldiers raging in Vilnius. Under the pressure of foreign countries and democratic forces in Russia, the Soviet leadership was forced to recognize Lithuania's right to independence.

In February 1991, a month after the tragic events of January, Iceland became the first foreign country to recognize Lithuania's independence. The Royal Embassy of Sweden was the first diplomatic mission opened in Vilnius. Independent Lithuania started its comeback into the world community.

↓ Ričardas Dailidė

↓ www.photostock.lt

↓ Klaudijus Driskius

⬈ The live chain That Lithuanians, Latvians, and Estonians formed by linking their hands together in August 1989 expressed the three countries' desire to be free and independent. The event called the Baltic Road connected Cathedral Square in Vilnius with Tompea Tower in Tallin.

⬉ The monument to Lenin removed from its pedestal in Lukiškių Square on August 23rd, 1991, was a token showing that Soviet ocupation would not return to Lithuania.

⬉ January 1991, was a dramatic time in the history of the Republic of Lithuania. As the Soviet military forcefully took over one state institution after another, tens of thousands people kept a round-the-clock watch of the Parliament Palace, the symbol of independence, ready to sacrifice themselves for freedom.

Antanas Smetona, the first President of the Republic of Lithuania from 1919 to 1920, resumed the position in 1926, and remained head until the country's occupation in 1940.

Aleksandras Stulginskis held the post of the country's head from 1922 to 1926.

Kazys Grinius was the President for less than a year in 1926.

Algirdas Brazauskas, the first President of Lithuania after it regained independence (1993-98).

Valdas Adamkus, a well-known environmentalist and a famous figure in the Lithuanian–American community, took over the country's helm in 1998.

In February 2003, Rolandas Paksas, the Republic of Lithuania's seventh president, took the helm of the state. Rolandas Paksas, an engineer by profession, was once famous as an ace at aerobatics. He is also an experienced politician who was the mayor of Vilnius and chairman of the Seimas.

The Presidency

The Office of the President of the Republic of Lithuania is situated in the very heart of Vilnius' Old Town, next to the University. Six hundred years ago here stood a house of the Franciscan monks that, later on, became the bishop's palace. In the early 19th century the palace was reconstructed and became the residence of the Russian tsar's Governor General

The president of the Republic of Lithuania is the head of state. He addresses the key issues of internal and foreign policy. The head of state, in accordance with the Constitution and the laws, appoints and discharges the prime minister, the cabinet members, the judges and other state officials. He is also in charge of the National Defense Council and is the commander-in-chief of the armed forces. The president signs international treaties of the Republic of Lithuania and the laws passed by the Seimas (parliament). If the head of state is temporarily abroad or falls ill, the chairman of the Seimas substitutes for him. In accordance with the current Constitution, the president is elected for a five-year term through direct ballot voting by the citizens of the Republic who are over 18 on election day. To be elected president of the Republic of Lithuania, one must be a citizen of Lithuanian extraction, not younger than 40, and prove that he or she has lived in Lithuania for the last three years. The same person cannot be elected president for more than two successive terms.

The heads of our country have always been prominent figures. Antanas Smetona was Lithuania's first president in 1919-1920, immediately after the institution was established. After a stipulation was included in the provisional constitution that the president be elected by the Seimas, its chairman, Aleksandras Stulginskis, occupied this position until elections. In 1922, the first Seimas elected A. Stulginskis as the country's president. The second Seimas also elected him as head of state. In 1926, A. Stulginskis was replaced by Kazys Grinius, who resigned on December 17 that same year. Two days later, A. Smetona was elected president for a second time. Unlike his predecessors, A. Smetona became the country's head as a result of a coup d'etat. A. Smetona was the country's president until 1940, when Lithuania was occupied by the Soviet Union, and the presidency was abolished.

All the Lithuanian presidents of the period between the two World Wars resided in the provisional capital of Kaunas, as Vilnius, along with neighboring areas, belonged to Poland at that time.

The institution of the president as the head of state was reestablished when the constitution was adopted by the referendum of October 25, 1992. The Democratic Labor Party won the elections that were held simultaneously with the referendum, and its leader, Algirdas Mykolas Brazauskas, was elected chairman of the Seimas and acted as president of the Republic of Lithuania until the presidential elections. In the elections of 1993, most of the voters cast their ballots in his favor, and A. Brazauskas became the first president of the restored, independent Republic of Lithuania. A. Brazauskas is a seasoned politician, who during the years of national revival consistently strove for the country's independence. Valdas Adamkus, a well-known figure in the Lithuanian-American community and a famous environmentalist, took over the helm of the state in 1998.

In February 2003, Rolandas Paksas, the Republic of Lithuania's seventh president, took the helm of the state. Rolandas Paksas, an engineer by profession, was once famous as an ace at aerobatics. He is also an experienced politician who was the mayor of Vilnius and chairman of the Seimas.

The flag of the country's president, the symbol of the head of state, is a rectangle of purple cloth. The coat of arms of Lithuania is depicted in its center, held by a griffon on the right, and a unicorn on the left.

The president's office moved to the splendid palace in the very heart of Vilnius' Old Town after Lithuania regained independence. Six hundred years ago, there stood a house of the Franciscan monks in this spot and, later on, the Bishop's Palace ace. In the early 19th century, the building was reconstructed in accordance with the design by the architect Vasily Stasov from St. Petersburg and became the residence of the Russian tsar's Governor General. The French emperor, Napoleon Bonaparte, stayed at this residence in 1812. Marshal J. Pilsudski lived here briefly at the beginning of the 20th century.

↑ www.photostock.lt

The Seimas of the Republic of Lithuania

The Seimas (parliament) is the legislative institution of the Republic of Lithuania. As early as the 15th century, the Seimas was the highest legislative body of the Grand Duchy of Lithuania, and later, that of the Republic of Poland as well.

After Lithuania was declared an independent state on February 16, 1918, the Council of Lithuania provided for elections to the Constituent Seimas, the guarantor of a democratic republic. The first general parliamentary election in the history of Lithuania was held on April 14-15, 1920. Over 90 percent of voters cast their ballots.

The Constituent Seimas accomplished its main objective – it drew up and adopted the Constitution of the State of Lithuania on August 1, 1922. On February 24, 1990, the Supreme Council was elected in accordance with the laws of the USSR. It was later renamed the Reconstituent Seimas. On March 11, 1990, the Reconstituent Seimas declared restoration of the independent Republic of Lithuania and secured its international recognition.

Since 1992, the Seimas of the Republic of Lithuania, in accordance with the country's constitution adopted by the citizens' general referendum of October 25, 1992, has been elected for a four-year term. Each of its 141 members is elected by voters' secret ballot. The Seimas, with a chairman in charge, debates, adopts and promulgates laws, approves or rejects candidates to the Prime Minister's (the head of the government's) position, supervises the government's activities, approves the national budget and controls adherence to it, imposes taxes, announces municipal elections, and ratifies international treaties of the Republic of Lithuania. The Seimas sets up committees to analyze draft laws. Permanent and ad hoc commissions deal with other important issues.

The office of the Seimas makes sure that the laws are passed in an efficient manner. It also sees to it that citizens can visit the most open institution of democratic power and during tours can familiarize themselves with the parliament's work, as well as meet the politicians they have elected.

EU membership

Lithuania has been striving to return to the family of European countries cherishing Western traditions of politics and culture since it restored independence in 1990

The signing of the European Union accession agreement in Athens on April 16, 2003, crowned the efforts of Lithuania that restored independence over a decade ago to return to the family of European nations and states cherishing Western traditions of politics and culture. On May 1, 2004, Lithuania is to become a member of this family enjoying full rights.

Now that the political agenda of the EU is becoming the political agenda of Lithuania, too, and our country's aspirations are becoming part of the aspirations and the objectives of the entire EU, a new phase begins: that of Lithuania's integration into Europe and its transatlantic insitutions, and that of continuous negotations in Brussels and the capitals of EU member states with an attempt to coordinate views and interests.

Our country is joining the EU as a motivated, reliable and constructive partner striving not only to benefit from the membership but also to contribute knowledge, experience and new ideas.

The referendum that was held in May 2003 clearly showed the wish and determination of our country's population to become part of democratic Europe, to efficiently use the opportunities offered by the membership, and to take an active part in planning and implementing the tasks and objectives of a united Europe.

Thousands of Lithuania's people expressed their hopes of a better life by participating in the events of EU accession referendum.

All political leaders of the country agitated for EU membership.

www.euro.lt

The EU Accession Agreement was signed in Athens on April 16, 2003, by Lithuanian Prime Minister A. Brazauskas, and Foreign Minister A. Valionis.

The Lithuanian Army

The nation's determination to maintain and defend the regained independence of the Lithuanian state has also created favorable conditions for restoring its army while cherishing the pre-war traditions and shaping new ones. Our army, created on the model of Western European military forces in regards to high standards of training and military requirements, is becoming strong and professional.

Throughout the world, the military remains an important tool of security policy. Threats still exist, and they are not confined within national borders; therefore, a new approach to the army is necessary. It is the quality of training and professional skills rather than numbers that ensure the successful performance of military forces.

A professional and motivated warrior is the greatest strength of the Lithuanian army. In the modern army, the warriors enjoy good conditions for carrying out service and for improving professional skills. Considerable attention is paid to develop soldiers as solid personalities and good citizens. A lot of officers and non-commissioned officers are studying military science abroad.

A mobile, well-trained military force that can be readily redeployed is the principal objective in developing the Lithuanian army. The military must always be ready to carry out peace-keeping operations, and, after Lithuania becomes a NATO member, to successfully perform in the collective system of defense and jointly with its allies to organize the country's defense.

NATO membership will not only guarantee independence and safety for Lithuania, but will also contribute to higher security within Eastern Europe as a whole. All for one, and one for all, the basic principle of the North Atlantic Treaty Organization, which for fifty-odd years has been the guarantor of security and stability of its members, will hold good for Lithuania as well. This attitude obligates Lithuania to be NATO's active and reliable partner, and its army to be ready to fulfill the tasks it is assigned in a professional manner.

Other countries think highly of our military, which for nearly a decade has been participating in operations supporting the efforts of the international community to restore peace in the Balkans and ensure security and stability in the Middle East. Since the first peace-keeping mission in former Yugoslavia, Lithuanian soldiers have been demonstrating high professional skills and the capability of carrying out important tasks. Our soldiers, while contributing to increased security and stability by preventing development of military conflicts and crises in the world, are also enhancing the security of Lithuania and its citizens.

The Grand Duke Algirdas Mechanized Infantry Battalion showed during exercises its readiness not only to defend the country but also participate in missions outside the boundaries of Lithuania. In the 21st century national and international security are closely related.

Military training and improvement of professional skills are the key factors in strengthening the army.

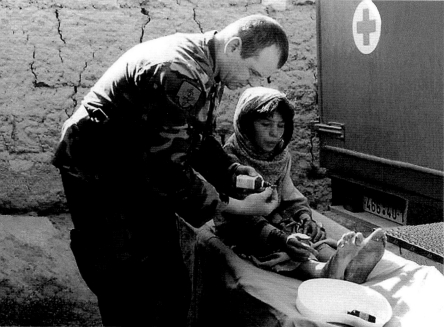

A Lithuanian military physician is rendering assistance to an Afghan girl. During the war the local population had no access to skilled medical aid for a long time.

Lithuania is an active member of international community. The country's military on a difficult and important peace-keeping mission in Kosovo maintains good relations with the locals.

↑ www.photostock.lt

The rulers we name our children after

The history of every nation has personalities whose glory does not wane, no matter how many centuries separate us from the period of time they lived in. The names of Mindaugas, Gediminas, and Vytautas, the rulers from the 13-15th ages, the time when the state was established and reached its greatest power, shine brightly in the history of Lithuania.

Mindaugas, the King of Lithuania

Grand Duke Mindaugas (r. 1238-63) is deservedly called the sovereign of Lithuania, the one who united numerous tiny duchies into a single state whose fame spread far to East and West. It is not known what lands Mindaugas reigned over before taking all the power into his hands. It cannot be said with certainty when Lithuania was united, either. It is obvious, however, that this happened before 1236 – the year when Mindaugas conducted negotiations with the Duke of Volyn as the ruler of the whole of Lithuania. Some of Mindaugas's competitors were killed in fighting, others, like Mindaugas's nephew, were sent off to govern other territories.

It also took considerable effort on Mindaugas's part to maintain the united state, as the dukes sent from their lands to faraway countries were not happy about it. Having made a treaty with regular enemies, the Livonian Order of Knights of the Cross and the Duchy of Volyn, they tried to overcome Mindaugas by laying siege to his castle, as told in ancient chronicles called Voruta, but fell short of their aim.

When, following the siege of Voruta, Mindaugas offered the Livonian Order peace, the Master of the Order demanded that Lithuania accept baptism. Mindaugas and his family were christened in 1250 or 1251. After the baptism, Mindaugas sent his emissaries to Rome to convey his loyalty to the Pope and ask for his protection. The Pope was also requested to crown Mindaugas king. In response, Pope Innocent IV declared Lithuania part of the realm of the Holy See on July 17, 1251, and authorized Henry, the Bishop of Chelmno, to crown Mindaugas king. Mindaugas and his wife, Morta, were crowned on July 6, 1253, and the Kingdom of Lithuania became part of the political system of Catholic Europe. The former Duke, now the King, strove to make his state stronger, and to modernize its structure. Nowadays, July 6 is formally celebrated as State Day. In 2003, a monument was unveiled to the King of Lithuania Mindaugas and a modern bridge connecting Old Town with New Vilnius was named after him when celebrating the 750th jubilee of the coronation of Mindaugas, one of the most prominent rulers of the country.

Gediminas, the founder of Vilnius

Legend has it that a dream prompted Gediminas, the Grand Duke of Lithuania, to build a castle on the hill at the confluence of the Neris and Vilnelė Rivers, and to set up the country's new capital at its foot. Tired after a successful hunt in the woods fringing the Šventaragis (Holy Horn) valley, the ruler slept that night at the foot of a hill. In his dream Gediminas saw an iron wolf standing on the hill and howling like a hundred wolves. Wise man Lizdeika, chief of all the pagan priests, interpreted the Duke's dream as follows: the iron-clad wolf atop the hill represented a castle and a town, the capital of Lithuania, which would appear there. The deafening howl of the wolf meant that the town's fame would spread far and wide.

Early in the 14th century, the Duke's dream came true. The town of Vilnius, at the confluence of two rivers that was mentioned in historical sources in 1323, is referred to as the capital of Lithuanian lands. The town was the first regular residence of Lithuania's rulers. The castle still called after Gediminas, became its heart.

Gediminas took great care of the Grand Duchy's new capital that at the time of his reign became the most important center of the state. It is known that the ruler wrote letters to the Pope and to important trade centers of the time. The head of a pagan state urged Christians not to be afraid to come to Lithuania. Gediminas promised to give land to warriors, craftsmen, and farmers, to exempt them from taxes for a ten-year period and to build churches. The ruler guaranteed the merchants free travel from one country to another without any taxes or duties.

The gothic red-brick tower of Gediminas Castle still gazes at Vilnius from the top of a tall hill. This is the best-preserved structure of the Upper Castle's defense complex that has become the symbol not only of the city but of the entire country as well.

Legendary Duke Vytautas, the king who was not crowned

The Grand Duke of Lithuania, Vytautas, whose merits to the medieval Lithuanian state cannot be overestimated, was to be crowned the second king in the history of the Grand Duchy of Lithuania in 1430. However, this was not to be. The messengers carrying the crown were captured, and Vytautas himself, who was eighty at the time, was badly injured when he fell off his horse. The ailing Vytautas the Great, worn out by political maneuvering, died at the end of October and was laid to rest in Vilnius Cathedral.

Vytautas, who reigned from 1392 to 1430, immediately after death became the most respected man of power in Lithuania. It was he who inscribed in gold letters the battle of Grünwald in the history of Lithuania. This battle brought the crusaders who had been ravaging the Baltic States for centuries to their knees. The Lithuanian nobility of the 15-16th centuries considered him a saint and a model to be emulated. The tradition of glorifying Vytautas has remained until today. In the 20th century Vytautas became the symbol of Lithuania and the struggle for recovering Vilnius from Poland. During Soviet times he was the historical figure that solidified the Lithuanians' national identity.

In 1930, when commemorating the 500th death anniversary of Vytautas the Great, oak trees, symbols of strength and tenacity, were planted in squares and parks in all large and small towns of Lithuania. Monuments to him were erected in many places. Some, say, in Perloja (Varėna District) survived the wars and the calamities of the Soviet period to remain until now. Most of the boys and girls born in 1930 were given the name of Vytautas and Vytautė. At present, Vytautas Clubs, functioning in nearly all districts of Lithuania, unite people having this name. They protect monuments dedicated to Vytautas and restore them, study the history of Lithuania and propagate it.

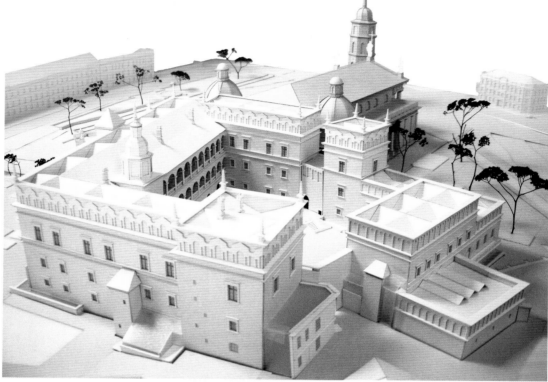

The Palace of Rulers of Lithuania, a part of the Lower Castle, is to be restored at the foot of the Gediminas Hill before the one-thousand-year anniversary of the mentioning of the name of Lithuania.

The millennium of Lithuania

The earliest mention of the name of Lithuania in written sources took place on February 14, 1009. The annals of the German town Quedlinburg contain information about the tragic end of the mission of St. Bruno of Querfurt, also known as Boniface, 'at the Russian-Lithuanian border'

For several years now Lithuania has been preparing to commemorate a very important date in its history. Although the 13th century, when Mindaugas ascended the throne, is usually considered to be the beginning of the Lithuanian state, the name of Lithuania was first mentioned in historical sources on February 14, 1009. The annals of the German town, Quedlinburg, contain information about the tragic end of the mission of St. Bruno of Querfurt, also known as Boniface, 'at the Russian-Lithuanian border' (in confinio Rusciae et Lituae).

One of the most important events commemorating the millennium of the first mention of the name of Lithuania will undoubtedly be the restoration of the Royal Palace of Vilnius Lower Castle at the foot of Gediminas Hill. The palace, constructed in the 14-17th centuries, was demolished by the tsar's order in 1799-1802.

During archaeological digs from 1987 to 2003, foundations of a Renaissance palace were discovered, along with remnants of cellars and of a gothic palace dating back to the 15th century. There were also fragments of fortifications of the Lower Castle, wooden structures, ramparts, moats, water canals, other architectural elements, utensils, and details of engineering mechanisms.

Suggestions to reconstruct the Royal Palace as the symbol of Lithuania's statehood had been made before, but only after the restoration of independent Lithuania did consistent implementation of the idea begin. The Directorate of Vilnius Castles is coordinating the work on investigation and restoration of the Royal Palace. The architects of the Design and Restoration Institute have developed the design of the reconstruction. Specialists of *Lietuvos pilys* (Lithuanian castles) Castle Research Center, and the Lithuanian Art Museum, scientists from Vilnius University, representatives of the Panevėžys Building Trust, *Geostatyba* and other organizations are contributing to the restoration, too.

The general public is also displaying interest in the restoration of the palace. The Fund to Support the Royal Palace not only accumulates funds, but is also striving to make the project known both in Lithuania and abroad. The World Community of Lithuanians has been actively supporting palace restoration.

Since ancient times, the Cathedral has been associated with the most memorable events of the state. It owes its present-day look to the famous architect of the turn of the 18th century, Laurynas Gucevičius.

St. Casimir's Chapel, artistically the most valuable specimen of early baroque, has been preserved in Vilnius's and Lithuania's most majestic architectural monument of classicism, the Cathedral.

Archcathedral-Basilica

The fresco remaining in the Cathedral's basement dating back to the 14-15th centuries is the oldest known mural in Lithuania.

The majestic classical Archcathedral-Basilica faces Gediminas Avenue, the main street of Vilnius. Presumably, it was built in the mid-13th century for the crowning of Mindaugas. After Mindaugas was killed, it became Perkūnas's (the pagan god Thunder's) temple.

After Lithuania accepted Christianity in 1387, Jogaila set up the Cathedral once again with the status of the principal house of prayer in Lithuania.

Since olden times the cathedral was associated with the most memorable events of the state. Here Vytautas the Great was solemnly crowned Grand Duke of Lithuania, and was buried as well. The remains of his wife, Duchess Ona, rest here, and so do those of some 8000 other prominent people. A silver casket with the relics of the only saint of Lithuania, Casimir, lies in the altar of St. Casimir's Chapel. The fresco remaining in the Cathedral's basements dating back to the 14-15th centuries is the oldest known mural in Lithuania.

The Cathedral that remembers many events had to be restored more than once. It was rebuilt in the gothic, Renaissance, and baroque styles. The building was last reconstructed in the late 17th century by the architect Laurynas Gucevičius. He created the most majestic monument of classicism in Vilnius and Lithuania as a whole from the cathedral that had been damaged by a fire, devastated by enemies, and struck by lightning, while preserving the artistically most valuable specimen of early baroque, St. Casimir's Chapel.

However, on the eve of the 19th century, major European empires were about to finish dividing among themselves the greatly weakened Grand Duchy of Lithuania. After the architect Laurynas Gucevičius died, his disciple, M. Schultz, finished rebuilding the edifice. He had three statues of saints erected above the frontal portico. The figure in the center is St. Helen with a gilded cross. The patron saint of Lithuania, Casimir, stands on her right, and St. Stanislaus is on her left.

During Soviet times, the statues were removed and the Cathedral was turned into a picture gallery. When it was returned to the faithful at the end of the 20th century, the statues resumed their places once again and today they gaze at the bustling capital of Lithuania that is becoming increasingly modern.

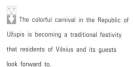

The colorful carnival in the Republic of Užupis is becoming a traditional festivity that residents of Vilnius and its guests look forward to.

The Republic of Užupis

Užupis, a historical suburb of Vilnius ascending a steep hill on the right bank of the Vilnia River, is one of the coziest and picturesque parts of Old Town. Writers, painters, actors and moviemakers are fond of it. For a long time, however, Užupis, mentioned in historical sources as early as the 16th century, was a poor section of town. Three bridges across the Vilnia connected it with the main part of the city.

Only a decade ago, Užupis was one of the most desolate quarters of Vilnius. It can be said that the revival of Užupis began when the idea occurred to Vilnius' artists to declare it an independent republic. It took just a few years to unrecognizably change Užupis. The colorful community of Užupis is being created by all its residents, from internationally recognized artists and young painters who live in their studios all year round to pragmatic businessmen and sundry eccentrics.

Onlookers throng to see the jovial procession and carnival on April 1st. The vigilantes of Užupis collect donations from them and stamp their passports with a special imprint of the Republic of Užupis.

On Christmas Eve, a traditional Firewood Market is arranged. Logs get chopped here, flea markets and auctions go into action, and actors and musicians perform. A welcoming address is given by those residents of the Republic of Užupis who are known for their merits in neighboring Vilnius, such as the capital's mayor, Artūras Zuokas. He was a journalist who became a businessman and, later, a politician. He was among the first to feel the magical charm and value of Užupis. He purchased an old dilapidated building (there was no other kind in Užupis) and had it restored.

Užupis is gradually becoming a respectable, residential area from whose yards picturesque views of Old Town unfold. Frequent outdoor events, shows of alternative fashion, and numerous informal art galleries have made Užupis one of the most active areas of Vilnius. The sculpture of an angel was erected in the main square on the initiative of the residents, symbolizing the revival of Užupis and welcoming visitors to this neighborhood.

Aušros Gate

Aušros Gate, one of the most frequented sights of Vilnius, was built by residents of Vilnius five centuries ago

When in 1503 the sovereign Alexander of the Grand Duchy of Lithuania ordered the residents of Vilnius to go to war, they were afraid to leave the town unprotected and asked him to be released from military service. In exchange, the townsfolk promised to encircle Vilnius with a wall and they kept their promise. The residents of the town themselves built the defensive wall and the gates leading into the town. The three-kilometer-long wall was completed in 1522. Medininkai or Aušros Gate was built in the southeastern part of the town, the part the invaders attacked most often.

For some time, the gate was called Krėva, or Medininkai Gate, because the road led to these towns. Later, the name Aštrieji Gate appeared, which is a Polish variation (the Poles still call it Ostra Brama). The Lithuanian name of Aušros Gate is derived from the old Lithuanian word *auštra*, or *aušra*, meaning dawn.

All the gates of the wall used to have patron saints. The Holy Virgin was chosen as the patron saint of Aušros Gate. In the 17th century, her picture that hung over the gate became famous as holy, and attracted crowds of Catholics, Unitarians, and the Russian Orhodox. The rumor that the picture worked miracles, fulfilled wishes of the faithful and redeemed sinners, spread widely over Eastern Europe. In 1927, the Pope allowed the solemn coronation of the icon of Aušros Gate, and gave it the name of the Virgin Mary, Mother of Compassion.

Modern research proves that the Virgin Mary's picture hanging in the Aušros Gate chapel was painted in the early 17th century. The picture, two meters high and more than a meter and a half wide, was painted in oil over eight oak boards joined together. 2,683 holes have been discovered in the picture that were made when the Virgin Mary's robes and symbols of her vows were nailed on.

Aušros Gate has withstood the test of time, and has recently become resplendent with new colors, restored by specialists from the Jondras Company.

The exquisite garment of the Virgin Mary, who gazes at the everyday life of the city from the heights of Aušros Gate, shines from afar. The garment was made of silver and then gilded by the goldsmiths of Vilnius. According to the fashion of old baroque, it was lavishly embellished with floral ornaments.

The icon of the Virgin Mary is not just a piece of art. The Roman Catholic Church also emphasizes its great importance. Pope John Paul II presented the Mother of Compassion with his cardinal's skullcap, and during his visit to Lithuania in 1993, he prayed in front of her picture.

Every newly appointed Bishop of Vilnius, before going to the Cathedral to assume his office, must pass through Aušros Gate and hail the miraculous picture. This tradition, begun in the 17th century, is still alive. The Cardinal of Lithuania, the Archbishop Metropolitan of Vilnius, Audrys Juozas Bačkis, also came to meditate and pray to the picture of the Virgin Mary before entering the Cathedral of Vilnius.

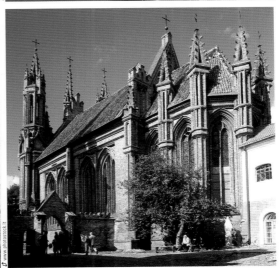

↑ Zenonas Nekrošius

♪ www.photostock.lt

♪ www.photostock.lt

↓ Robertas Kananavičius (26-27)

Bricks of nearly forty different shapes were used for the faëade of the building.

When St. Anne's Church was last renovated almost a hundred years ago, architectural elements characteristic of neo-gothic architecture appeared in its interior.

A gothic masterpiece in Vilnius

A closer look at the façade of St. Anne's Church reveals the so-called pillars of the Royal House of Gediminas, the ancient coat of arms of Lithuania's rulers

In comparison with gothic buildings of worship in France or Germany, St. Anne's Church is elegant and light, rather than majestic or monumental. This is why it fascinates both people of Lithuania and tourists visiting the country.

According to legend, an eminent architect was building the Bernardine Church nearby whereas his disciple was constructing St. Anne's. When the two buildings were almost finished, everyone saw that the disciple's church was more beautiful. Burning with revenge, the teacher pushed the gifted disciple from a tall scaffold.

It is believed that the architect Mykolas Eukingeris built St. Anne's Church at the turn of the 15th century. He decided to build with brick while retaining the traditional style reserved for wooden buildings. The daring and creative architect used bricks of nearly forty different shapes for the façade of the building. Folks joke that he inscribed letters and designs of twisted ropes with bricks. As a matter of fact, a closer look at the façade of St. Anne's Church does reveal the so-called pillars of the Royal House of Gediminas, the ancient coat of arms of Lithuania's rulers.

The church burned down during the fire of 1564, but it took a relatively short time, sixteen years, to rebuild and consecrate it. For a while St. Martin's fraternity, comprised of Germans and other Catholics from abroad, utilized the church that had been restored to life. Somewhat later, the church became a forum for the Reformation. Today it is still open to all the faithful.

As years went by, St. Anne's Church preserved its incomparable charm. The story has it that Napoleon, on his way to Russia in 1812, stayed for a while in Vilnius and was bewitched by the church's beauty. The famous general allegedly expressed a wish to put it on his palm and take it back to Paris. However, bitter historical truth differs: Napoleon ordered St. Anne's Church to be turned into a warehouse during the war with Russia where military supplies and prisoners of war were kept.

Renovation last touched St. Anne's Church almost a hundred years ago. It was then that architectural elements characteristic of neo-gothic architecture appeared in its interior.

New Vilnius

Vilnius is becoming a modern business center of the Baltic region. New Western-looking office buildings have been springing up, hotels are being refurbished and new ones constructed. Business, entertainment, and sports centers are opening their doors

Some 600,000 residents live in present-day Vilnius, which occupies an area of ca. 400 square kilometers. Commercial banks and branches of foreign banks, the National Stock Exchange of Lithuania, insurance and stock-brokerage companies are operating in the country's capital. Internet and SMS banking services are being provided in the city, the ATM network has been developed, and one can pay for vehicle parking by sending an SMS message. Research, design, and technology centers employing highly skilled specialists have been fast developing.

The city is becoming a modern business center in the Baltic region. In 2003, the reconstruction of the main thoroughfare, Gediminas Avenue, was completed, and a modern bridge named after King Mindaugas started connecting the right and left banks of the Neris River. New Western-looking office buildings have been springing up, hotels are being refurbished and new ones constructed, business, entertainment, and sports centers are opening their doors. FORUM PALACE, a building of unique architectural decisions, rising in terraces from the surroundings and the façade, replicating the bend of the river nearby, begins a row of buildings in the business triangle on the right bank of the Neris. The concise and simple oval of the FORUM PALACE, equally significant from all sides, abounds in glass. It creates the impression of being open to its surroundings and allows a great view of the city's panorama. The FORUM PALACE divided into zones is an entire micro-world where business, entertainment and recreation go hand in hand, and the visitor can choose an activity to his or her liking.

The city that produces nearly a third of the country's GDP, has been attracting businessmen's attention. Telecommunications, trade in petroleum products, building materials and pharmaceutical industries attract the bulk of foreign investment. Sweden, Denmark, Estonia, the USA, the United Kingdom, Finland, and Germany are the major investors. Clothes, electric devices, textiles, machine tools and mechanical equipment, wood and merchandise made of wood, high-precision instruments and leatherware are the capital's staple exports.

The fast-growing capital of Lithuania is open to all those willing to set up their business companies and being equal partners in creating the vision of Vilnius as a prospering, European city.

Visitors are welcome

Cities that are becoming more modern from day to day, small towns that have preserved the ancient spirit, sincere people, picturesque nature, delicious food, and good roads – these are the advantages tourists to Lithuania mention most often. However, they spend most of their time in Vilnius. Surveys show that some 80 per cent of those coming to Lithuania visit its capital. Over 600,000 foreign guests stayed in Vilnius in 2002 – nearly one fifth more than in 2001.

Most tourists come from Poland, Russia, Germany, Latvia, and the Scandinavian countries. Increasingly more arrive from the United Kingdom, Austria, Holland, Belgium, Luxemburg, France, Spain, Italy, Portugal, Turkey, Greece, Ireland, Iceland, Eastern European countries, and Canada every year. They are attracted by Old Town with its wonderful buildings of gothic, Renaissance, baroque and classical styles, picturesque views, original and cozy atmosphere, as well as intense cultural life with numerous festivals, holidays and concerts.

During the nearly month-long Days of the Capital, masquerades and fairs, events organized by artists, and exhibitions attract many visitors from abroad. The capital's guests like visiting the Modern Art Center, the National Gallery, and the Philharmonic Society Hall. Foreigners whose first acquaintance with Vilnius often takes place during the city's culture days abroad (in Gdansk, Berlin, Erfurt or Prague), are also glad to come to Vilnius.

The sector of tourist services is being fast developed in the city. New, modern hotels offering facilities necessary for businessmen have been opened. Many of them have halls for conferences and seminars. Vilnius now boasts numerous restaurants, cafes, clubs, casinos, an ice palace, and indoor tennis courts. A Vilnius City Card has been issued. Its holder is entitled to visit the capital's museums, restaurants, and clubs free of charge or at a discount.

The rapidly expanding network of hotels in Vilnius and the growing number of visitors to tourist information offices attest that arrivals to the country's capital are on the increase.

The capital of the Republic of Lithuania, Vilnius, is the country's largest city situated at the confluence of the Vilnia and Neris Rivers. Old Town, the historical center of Vilnius, occupies an area of 360 hectares and is one of the largest in Eastern Europe. Some fifteen hundred buildings of Old Town remain from different ages, therefore all architectural styles of Europe intertwine here. Although Vilnius is sometimes referred to as a town of baroque, buildings of gothic, Renaissance, and classical styles can be found here, too.

Old Town of the Lithuanian capital, carefully maintained, restored and cherished, is called the architectural pearl of Eastern Europe. In recognition of its international importance, UNESCO included it in 1994 in its list of World Heritage Sites.

Gediminas Tower and Cathedral Square are the key elements, like representational gates leading to the historical center of the capital. The main tourist routes begin here, leading along Pilies (Castle) Street towards Aušros Gate. In the 13th century, the Lower Castle stood in Cathedral Square, called Šventaragis Valley in ancient chronicles and legends. The castle housed the administrative and defense center of the Grand Duchy of Lithuania, an arsenal, and religious institutions. The belfry tower that still looms in the square was once a gothic defense tower behind which the Vilnelė River flowed. The streets of the town founded in 1323 wound their way among noblemen's and landlords' houses, workshops of craftsmen, dividing it into small, irregular squares. In later times, larger quarters squeezed into the network of narrow streets. Christian and Russian Orthodox churches, synagogues, Reformers' prayer houses, and Karaite kenessas stand here side by side.

Old Vilnius

Medininkai or Aušros Gate, leading to castles of southern Lithuania, is one of the most impressive structures remaining to this day. Highly valued are also St. Theresa's Church, the gothic Church of St. Anne, the architectural ensemble of Bernardines, the building of the Philharmonic Society Hall, and many others.

The Town Hall and the square in front of it was the place around which all town life was centered. Didžioji (Big) Street leading up to it is one of the oldest in Vilnius.

The Hill of Three Crosses in the vicinity of Gediminas Castle, once called Plikasis (Bald) or Kreivasis (Crooked) Hill, on which the wooden Kreivoji Castle stood ready to defend the dwellers of the town and its suburbs, has become another symbol of Vilnius. The old buildings of the University with the majestic St. John's Church are the pride of Old Town. The unique ensemble that took three centuries to build, combines elements of gothic, Renaissance, baroque, and classical architecture. Inside the buildings of different epochs joined together, there are thirteen courtyards of varying sizes. The most important of these is Didysis (Large), acting as a pantheon perpetuating the memory of the University's founders, donors, and prominent scholars.

Not all the buildings of old Vilnius withstood the passage of centuries, and its streets were straightened out. Nevertheless, in the 21st century, just like many centuries before, business and art, different religions and cultures continue to go hand in hand.

Kaunas

Kaunas, still taking pride at once being Lithuania's provisional capital, is the most Lithuanian and the safest of the country's cities

Kaunas is situated in the heart of Lithuania, at the confluence of its two largest rivers, the Nemunas and the Neris. A 9th century settlement some two hundred years later grew into the town of Kaunas which connected East with West for all times.

The growth of Kaunas is associated with Vytautas, the Grand Duke of Lithuania. The ruler often visited the town and entertained foreign guests there. Hansa merchants set up warehouses in Kaunas in the 15th century, as it was in a strategically convenient location, and encouraged the town's development. In the 16th century, Kaunas was reconstructed on the model of European cities. In the early 19th century, Napoleon with his army crossed the Nemunas in the vicinity of Kaunas. Later on, Adomas Mickevičius (Adam Mickiewicz), the great Polish-Lithuanian poet, taught at a school in Kaunas's Old Town. C. Sugihara, the Japanese diplomat who worked in Kaunas during World War II, saved the lives of thousands of Jews.

When in 1920 Vilnius and the neighboring regions were occupied by the Poles, Kaunas became the provisional capital of Lithuania and once again enjoyed a period of prosperity. Vytautas Magnus University was founded, a large community of intelligentsia formed in the town, and the country's first theaters and museums opened their doors.

Kaunas is the most Lithuanian of all towns: over 80 percent of its residents are Lithuanians. There are six universities and as many other higher schools of learning. The bulk of nearly 400,000 of Kaunas residents are in school, studying, or teaching others. Statistics show that Kaunas is the safest of Lithuania's cities.

The pride of the city is the Town Hall Square where in the center the Kaunas Town Hall stands in splendor. Surrounded by merchants' and craftsmen's houses dating back to the 15-16th centuries, the place used to be called Market Square. Nowadays it is a popular venue for the city's cultural events.

The Resurrection Church in the provisional capital was constructed as a symbol of national revival and hope. All the efforts of the occupational Soviet power to erase the symbol from the people's memory were in vain. Now the church is being reconstructed with people's donations. AB *Kausta* Company is carrying out the reconstruction.

The interior of the largest building in Kaunas' Old Town, the 15-th-century gothic Arch-cathedral, is one of the most interesting in Lithuania. The church is decorated with numerous paintings and pieces of architecture.

The funicular in Aleksotas is the oldest means of transport of this type in Lithuania. Still authentic, for 70 years it has been taking people atop Aleksotas Hill, the best vantage point overlooking the city center and Old Town.

Kaunas is open to friends and cooperation partners. The city is becoming a major industrial center again. International corridors of motor transport intersect here and railway arteries intermingle. Water transport is also making a comeback. Karmėlava Airport, situated in the vicinity of the city, is capable of accepting and servicing the largest airliners.

Savanorių (Volunteers') Avenue, the city's fastest-changing thoroughfare, is becoming a link joining the two historical capitals, Kaunas and Vilnius. Next to the Resurrection Church nearby, the Žaliakalnis Center of Culture, Education and Business will appear shortly. Major centers of logistics have started functioning in other parts of the city, another proof that Kaunas is a town convenient for investment.

The name of Kaunas can also be found in the lists of international cultural events. The prestigious International Festival of Music that is held every summer at Pažaislis on the initiative of the Kaunas State Choir, well known in many continents, is distinguished by famous performers. In spring, the Kaunas Jazz festival attracts jazz fans from all over the world. The Days of Kaunas in late May, the event celebrating the city's birthday, is becoming an impressive holiday. For several years now music lovers have gathered for the concerts of a traditional operetta festival that takes place near the old Castle of Kaunas. The city boasts numerous sights, such as M. K. Čiurlionis Art Museum, the Picture Gallery, the galleries of A. Žmuidzinavičius's works and his collection of devils, the museums of pharmacy, jewels, etc. the city has a sufficient number of hotels as well as clubs and restaurants offering excellent service and cultural programs.

△ Stuccowork is one of the most
impressive details of the interior.

Near the Kaunas Sea, on the outskirts of the town, shines the pearl of 17th century Lithuanian baroque: the architectural ensemble of Pažaislis.

The history of Pažaislis goes back to 1660, when Christopher Zigmantas Pacas, the Great Chancellor of the Grand Duchy of Lithuania, founded a monastery and a church to commemorate his only son who had died. The buildings were designed and built by brilliant masters of baroque, architects G. B. Frediani, and C. and P. Putinis. M. A. Palloni from Florence painted more than a hundred frescoes, and the stuccowork was done by sculptors from Lombardy.

Camaldolese monks took care of the Pažaislis ensemble, the monastery and The Church of the Virgin Mary's Visitation, since its establishment in 1831.

In 1920, nuns from the USA founded the still functioning St. Casimir's Sisters' Nunnery in Pažaislis.

Women were not allowed to enter Pažaislis Church or other houses of prayer belonging to Camaldolese monks. The tall walls of the monastery, an alley with a front yard and spacious courtyards, separated the hermitic shelters of the Camaldolese from the world. The remains of A. Lvov, the author of the Russian national anthem, rest in one of the courtyards.

Camaldolese monks accumulated a great number of art works in the Pažaislis Monastery. One of the most valuable exhibits is the picture of the Virgin Mary with the infant, known as *The Mother of Beautiful Love*. Pope Alexander VII presented it to the founder of Pažaislis, C. Z. Pacas, who hung it in the church. During Soviet times, the picture was stowed away in the Kaunas Cathedral. It was returned to the restored church of Pažaislis about ten years ago.

Pažaislis

The history of
Pažaislis goes back
to 1660

Another priceless piece of art is a cycle of eleven pictures painted in the monastery's corridor depicting the mission of St. Bruno of Querfurt to baptize pagan Lithuania. It is believed to be the earliest and probably the only piece of art describing in detail the events of 1009, when the name of Lithuania was first mentioned.

It is impossible to imagine summer in Pažaislis without music. Since 1996, a musical festival that has received international acclaim takes place here annually. An audience as large as 30,000 attends the concerts of the festival. *Philharmonie der Nationen*, (Germany), BBC Philharmonic Orchestra, (the UK), the Moscow Soloists' Chamber Orchestra, *Camerata*, (St. Petersburg), have all performed at festivals in Pažaislis. Yury Bashmet's alto, Alexander Kniazev's cello, Petras Geniušas's piano, have been heard here. The German soprano, Teresa Seidl, and the British tenor, Neil Mackie, sang in Pažaislis. The legend of the music world, conductor Yehudi Menuhin, honored the Pažaislis festival more than once.

▽ Wonderful baroque architecture is
the fascinating feature of the monastery.

Klaipėda

Klaipėda, the city that has celebrated its 750th anniversary, now is not only Lithuania's gate to the world but also one of the country's most successfully developing regions

Founded in 1252, Klaipėda is distinct from other cities of Lithuania with its specific architecture of Old Town, characteristic of Western European towns. Its history began when Eberhardt von Sein, the Master of the Livonian Order, had a wooden castle built at the top of a hill on the Danė River bank. The town of Memel then rose around Memelburg Castle on the shores of the Baltic Sea and the Curonian Lagoon. The Lithuanian name of the town, Klaipėda, was first mentioned in 1420. Since the 13th century, the Germans, *kuršiai*, and Lithuanians lived here side by side. In later ages, Scottish, English, and other nationalities diversified the multilingual panorama of the city.

In the early 19th century, the city was briefly made the capital of Prussia. The King of Prussia, Frederick Wilhelm III, lived with his wife Louise in the Town Hall building on the present-day Danės Street for nearly a year. At that time, the Act on Abolition of Serfdom in the Kingdom of Prussia was announced in Klaipėda.

The city today is Lithuania's gate to the seas. This is a fast growing industrial and transport center, attractive to foreign investment, production and business as well as to collaboration with other ports of Europe and other continents. As highways and sea routes intersect here, the main administration institutions, enterprises and organizations of the country's sea business are concentrated in Klaipėda.

Economically, the city is one of the most successfully developing regions in Lithuania. At the same time, it is one of the most important recreation and tourism sites. A terminal for passenger ships was opened in 2003 in the center of the city not far away from the castle site. In preparation for a developing cruise business, the port of Klaipėda has joined the *Cruise Europe* international organization.

Klaipėda, Lithuania's only seaport, is the country's third largest city. Extending in length for 15 kilometers along the shore of the Curonian Lagoon in a 2-3 kilometer-wide strip, it occupies an area of over 98 square kilometers, and has a population of some 193,000. The Danė River flowing across the city splits it in two, the present-day city center on the right bank, and a small Old Town on the left. In the ice-free seaport situated in the western part of the city the horns of fishing and freight vessels from around the globe blast all year round.

The specific architecture of Old Town characteristic of Western European cities is a feature that distinguishes Klaipėda from other towns of Lithuania.

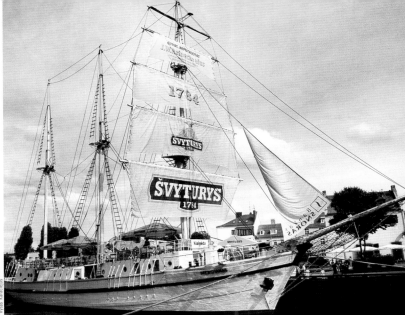

The seaport town is a cultural center of Western Lithuania. Some ten years ago, a university was founded here. The city boasts a drama and musical theater. In summer, the Castle Jazz Festival, the Sea Festival and other events are held here.

The residents of Klaipėda and visitors alike consider the sailing vessel *Meridianas* the symbol of the city. The ship that was once used for training seamen and for sailing on long voyages, was moored to the Danė River embankment over three decades ago and became one of the most popular restaurants of this seaport town.

The Sea Museum of Lithuania established in Kopgalis, the northernmost point of the Curonian Spit, long ago became one of the favorite sites frequented by residents of Klaipėda and visitors to the seaside. The marine flora and fauna in the museum are combined with an exposition of the history of seamanship. An ethnographic fisherman's farmstead has been built at the site of an old fishing village. Exhibited next to it are fishing vessels, the predecessors of modern Lithuanian commercial fishing ships. Together with the Sea Museum and Aquarium they form a unique complex that allows a closer look at the sea.

Every summer weekend the largest pool of the dolphinarium, 5.5 meters deep and with a capacity of 1300 cubic meters, resounds with the applause of the audience when trained animals, dolphins and sea lions, give a show together with a team of synchronized swimmers, dancers and acrobats.

Meridianas, a three-masted sailing ship known as the symbol of Klaipėda, was built in 1948. For a long time it was used as a training ship for the Navigation School. Later it was rebuilt and sailed to distant destinations until in 1971 it was moored to the Danė River embankment and became one of the most popular restaurants of the seaport town.

A fountain with the sculpture of Anikė and bas-relief of German poet Simon Dach stands in the square of the Drama Theater. Professor Simon Dach was born in Klaipėda in the 17th century and worked at the local university. The girl Anikė is a character in a poem by S. Dach steeped in romantic stories. Therefore it is no coincidence that residents of Klaipėda have rendezvous in the Theater Square.

← Vytas Karaciejus   ↑ Vytas Karaciejus

Sea Festival

The Sea Festival that goes on for several days has become a traditional event people are looking forward to more eagerly than to any other. About one million people who are sure they see a vestige of a sailor's striped shirt beneath their street clothes come to the festival every year

🔲 The Danė River splits the city in two, the present-day city center on the right bank, and a small Old Town on the left.

On the last weekend in July, tens of thousands of people gather in Klaipėda, Lithuania's seaport. They are attracted by the Sea Festival, a colorful event held there every year. Some 50,000 guests, more than there were residents in Klaipėda, came to the first Sea Festival that was arranged in 1934 and in which the country's President took part. It was then that one of the most beautiful traditions of the festival – paying homage to those who perished at sea – was established.

Nowadays the country's highest officials, foreigners, let alone hundreds of thousands of Lithuanians try not to miss the three-day-long event. Since 1994, Sea Day has been officially recognized as a commemorative day in Lithuania.

What makes the merry Sea Festival such a success? Most probably the daring of the organizers who do not hesitate to place the city at the participants' disposal. Everyone is given an opportunity to create, to unburden one's heart, in short, to act as one wishes and to let his or her imagination run wild.

The audiences are delighted by the skill of prominent performers from Lithuania and abroad. They are touched by sincere tunes of street musicians, and admire the artifacts displayed by folk artists. The organizers, assisted by the ruler of the seas, Neptune, who sails down the Danė River, remind the public of the significant role of the sea in the history of civilization, and about maritime traditions. During the Sea Festival of 2003 that was held with the motto "Moor your boat in Klaipėda", a cruise ship terminal was opened.

If beneath your street clothes you see a vestige of a sailor's striped shirt, start getting ready for a trip to Klaipėda. The initiators of the festival turn the whole city into a large ship on the last day with an impressive carnival. In its messhall and holds, on its decks – in the town squares, streets, and in the water – there will always be enough room and events for everyone.

The sea beneath the window

One of the most popular traditions among holidaymakers in Palanga is watching the sun set. The impressive sight of the sun setting in the sea entices one to see it again and again

Palanga is the largest resort of Lithuania situated near the Baltic Sea. Although it was first mentioned in written sources as early as 1253, it became a real resort only in the late 19th century, when the Tiškevičius' Counts had complexes of summer cottages built, a summer theater established, paths made for promenades in the forest, and baths with marble tubs and heated water constructed here. In 1882, the Tiškevičius brothers ordered a wooden bridge built leading into the sea. Eventually the bridge became one of the main symbols of the resort of Palanga. At the beginning of the 20th century, Palanga was in no way inferior to the best resorts of Germany, and its beaches were ordered according to the best foreign fashion of the day.

Palanga became the unofficial summer capital of Lithuania during its period of independence. An airport was also built during this period between the two World Wars to meet the needs of the resort.

The old resort of Palanga has been growing larger and more modern at a brisk pace. Now it stretches for 25 kilometers along the Baltic Sea coast and is divided into three parts, old, new, and Šventoji – many believe the latter to be an individual settlement. In the 2003 season, the beach of the Botanical Park of Palanga was granted a Blue Flag certificate.

Numerous events are held in Palanga all year round. Crowds of people fond of bathing in winter and dubbing themselves seals, flock to Palanga in February for the Seals of Palanga holiday to take a dip in the ice-cold Baltic. Early June marks the beginning of the summer holiday season. Concerts are given as well as street shows; discotheques, sports competitions, a craftsmen's fair and numerous other events take place crowned by impressive fireworks at the sea bridge.

Since 1970, Night Serenades, wonderful soirees of classical music, take place in late July on the Tiškevičius' manor grounds.

One of the oldest and best known traditions of Palanga is watching the sun set from the pedestrian bridge over the sea. The bridge, devastated by waves and rebuilt again several times (in 1923, 1968, 1991, and 1997), the Birutė and Naglis hills, the Botanical Park, and the Tiškevičius' manor with its collection of amber are the principal sights of Lithuania's most important sea resort.

The pedestrian bridge in Palanga, restored a few times and moved somewhat southwards in 1997, still remains as popular as in the past. A jetty for passenger ships has been constructed on its southern side, and platforms for anglers on the northern and eastern parts where the bridge curves.

The pedestrian bridge in Palanga, restored a few times and moved somewhat southward in 1997, still remains as popular as in the past. A jetty for passenger ships has been constructed on its southern side, and platforms for anglers on the northern and eastern parts where the bridge takes a turn.

↑ Antanas Varanka

www.palanga.lt

43

↑ Romualdas Požerskis

Curonian Spit

The unique landscape of the Curonian Spit is not cherished by sole Lithuania anymore. Since 2000, the National Park of the Curonian Spit has been put on the UNESCO list of the world heritage, classified under cultural landscape values

Kuršių Nerija (Curonian Spit), the long, narrow, sandy peninsula separating Kuršių Lagoon from the Baltic Sea, is ideally suitable for recreation. The northern 52-kilometer-long section of the peninsula, whose overall length is 100 kilometers with a width ranging from 400 meters to 4 kilometers, belongs to Lithuania. The landscape of the Curonian Spit is unique: dunes covered with scarce vegetation, and a forest growing in sandy soil, mostly of pines and mountain pines planted by man, in which elk, roe-deer, wild boar, foxes and hares roam freely.

To preserve the unique nature and to tame the elements, residents formed protective foredunes a good hundred years ago and planted conifers on the shifting sand hills that had buried fourteen fishermen's villages. Now some 900 plant species grow on the Curonian Spit, many of which have been entered into Lithuania's Red Book. Ten-odd years ago the National Park of the Curonian Spit was established with the intention of preserving the coastal landscape. In 2000, UNESCO included the park in its list of World Heritage Sites as a valuable cultural landscape.

The summer season in Kuršių Nerija opens in late May. Holidaymakers yearning for quiet choose the picturesque villages of Juodkrantė, Pervalka and Preila. Those hungering for thrills go to bustling Nida. They are drawn by the clear water of the Baltic Sea, the wind-blown dunes, and the generous sun, which shines here nearly two thousand hours a year, longer than in any other part of Lithuania. Numerous interna-

⊳ Small resort towns of the Curonian Spit abound in ethnographic farmsteads and fishermen's huts.

↓ Romualdas Požerskis

⊳ The peninsula runs for nearly a hundred kilometres with its width varying from 400 meters to 4 kilometres.

↓ Vytautas Karaciejus

In the Curonian Lagoon one can still see sailing *kurėnas*, an authentic fishing boat from the 16th-17th centuries. As a rule, these flat-bottomed sailboats used to be made of oak planks. They were up to 10 meters long and 3 meters wide. It would take skilful craftsmen of Gilija a month to build a *kurėnas*, and it cost as much as a wooden house.

Wooden monuments carved from a single plank used to be called *krikštas*. These were placed in graveyards and cemeteries of Lithuania Minor and Samogitia since the early 16th century. The tradition gradually died out. Unlike Catholic crosses, *krikštas* used to be erected at the foot of the grave. *Krikštases* of different kinds of wood and ornaments decorated female and male graves.

tional art and classical music festivals among other festive events are also an attraction.

A cultural center named after the famous German writer, Thomas Mann, a Nobel prize winner who spent several summers with his family in Nida, organizes international conferences, seminars and other events every year. An exhibition hall has been equipped in a wooden-framed cottage built on the shore of Curonian Lagoon. Representatives of different fields of art live and work here in summer. Nida's Jazz Marathon is becoming increasingly popular, and a summer festival of chamber music attracts much attention.

People discovered the Curonian Spit ten thousand years ago. Its first inhabitants were hunters, who in small parties wandered in pursuit of reindeer and elk. Fixed settlements in Neringa appeared in the fourth millennium B.C. As recently as a hundred and fifty years ago, the inhabitants of the peninsula earned their living primarily by fishing. It was only in the mid-19th century that holidaymakers started bringing in profit. Juodkrantė was the first fishermen's village that was turned into a resort. Some time later, artists and vacationers started showing interest in Smiltynės Kopgalis, Preila and Pervalka.

▶ Visitors to the Museum of Amber that forty years ago opened its doors in the former palace of Count Tiškevičius in Palanga can see 4500 exhibits today.

▶ Ąžuolas Leonas Vaitukaitis is one of the artists who use amber as a means to express creativity.

▶▶ The Museum of Amber prides itself on the so-called Stone of the Sun, a piece of amber weighing 3.526 kg.

Gold of the Baltic Sea

The tribes that lived on the Baltic Sea coast five thousand years ago gathered amber and used it for producing ornaments

According to legend, there once stood an amber palace of incomparable beauty at the bottom of the Baltic Sea. The ruler of the palace, the goddess Jūratė, fell in love with Kastytis, a fisherman rescued during a storm. The goddess's love for an ordinary mortal caused the wrath of Perkūnas (Thunder). He smashed Jūratė's amber palace, and chained Kastytis to a rock at the bottom of the sea. Now only pieces of amber that waves throw onto the Baltic shore, remnants of Jūratė's palace, remind us of this love story.

Amber was first mentioned in written sources (Assyrian cuneiform) in the 10th century B.C. Amber, also known as the gold of the Baltic Sea, is fossilized pine resin. Approximately 50 million years ago, when luxuriant subtropical forests grew in southern Scandinavia and in the area of the present-day Baltic Sea, the resin flowed out of resiniferous pines that later became extinct. The resin hardened, rolled to the ground and eventually turned into amber. Rivers carried the amber forming deposits between the present-day Kaliningrad region, Poland, and southern Sweden. The deposits remain until today. The sea usually washes ashore only small pieces, weighing 100-300 grams. The largest lumps weigh 6-10 kilograms. They are kept in museums of different countries. As a rule, amber is yellow, less often white, bluish, green or brown. Once in a while, tiny plants or insects are found in hardened pine resin. A piece of amber can contain a reptile's slough, a swarm of mosquitoes, centipedes, bees and ants. Amber with such inclusions is highly valued by scientists and collectors. The Museum of Amber opened in the palace of Count Feliksas Tiškevičius in Palanga forty years ago, boasts a large number of specimens with inclusions. Now there are 4,500 exhibits in the museum, from natural pieces of amber to decorations dating back to the Stone Age, as well as works by modern artists. Approximately five times more specimens are stored in the museum's depositories. The pride of the Museum of Amber in Palanga is the so-called Stone of the Sun, weighing 3.526 kilograms.

The tribes that lived on the Baltic Sea coast more than five thousand years ago carved amulets and ornaments out of gathered amber. Later on, they started trading it for salt and bronze. During the times of the Roman Empire amber decorations connected the Balts and other tribes of the Baltic Sea region with the ancient civilizations. Two thousand years ago amber reached present-day Greece and Italy along the Amber Road running through Europe.

Nowadays decorations, cigarette-holders, boxes and other artifacts made by the best amber craftsmen from Juodkrantė, Šventoji and Palanga are taken all the way to Russia, Western Europe, and North America.

▶ Scientists and collectors highly value amber with inclusions.

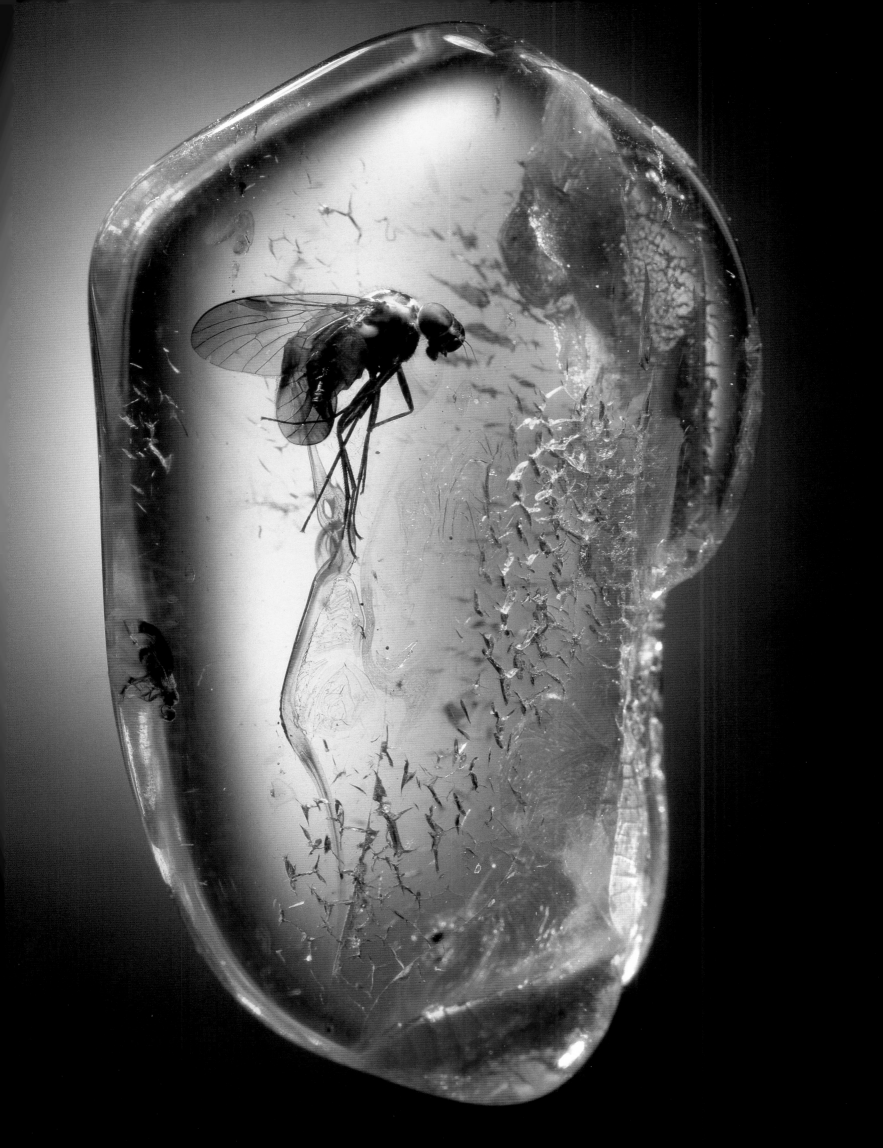

↑ Klaudijus Driskius

Kernavė

Kernavė reveals its beauty in summer time, when all kinds of holidays and folklore festivals are held. Rasa (St. John's Day) festival was first organized here as early as 1967, later to become a tradition

The ancestors of modern Lithuanians settled in the Pajauta valley, in the vicinity of a picturesque crook of the Neris River, ten thousand years ago. They named the riverside that used to grow soggy during fall showers and spring thaws: Kernavė. In old Lithuanian, the word meant a low, wet place. During the 13-14th centuries at the foot of hill-forts, a medieval town grew there with a population of 3-4 thousand. It was a major political and strategic center at the initial stages of the formation of the Lithuanian state. One of the most important castles of King Mindaugas is believed to have stood there.

The significance of Kernavė grew even more during the reign of Grand Duke Traidenis (r. 1269-82). Here he set up his residence from which he led the army that assaulted Russian and Polish lands, and fought against crusaders. The town's merchants maintained active trade contacts with neighboring countries. However, in the 14th century the prosperous town gave up under the continuous onslaught of crusaders. In 1390, while running for their lives from these assailants, the local residents set fire to their native town and abandoned it. Since then Kernavė forever lost its grandeur. Five mounds like giant brothers loom today close to one another surrounding the provincial town. Lithuania proposes that UNESCO include the mounds in its list of World Heritage sites. A pagan temple is believed to have stood on the Altar Hill, the oldest mound, situated in the middle. The Oracle Lizdeika, chief of all the pagan priests, who interpreted the prophetic dream of Grand Duke Gediminas, kindled his fire and predicted the future to the end of his days.

According to legend, an underground road used to run below the other four mounds, those of Lizdeika, Kriveikiškės, Mindaugas' Throne, and Castle (also known as Garrison Hill). It connected Kernavė with Trakai and Vilnius. One could get onto the road through a bronze door in Kernavė, a silver door in Trakai, and a golden door in Vilnius. After thieves stole the bronze door, the road opened up and oxen of the townsfolk of Kernavė entered the tunnel. The owners found the missing cattle only towards evening. The locals were afraid lest some evildoers should find the secret passage and blocked it up with earth. Nobody has set foot in it since.

The beauty of Kernavė is revealed in summer time when various festivities and folklore festivals take place. As early as 1967, Rasų (Dew, or St. John's) Day was celebrated here. Eventually, the celebration became traditional. During the festivities, ancient rites are performed, people dance and sing. At night, bonfires and hubs of wheels are burned on the mounds. At the break of dawn, homage is paid to the sun.

Every year, the 6th of July (on this day Mindaugas was crowned the King of Lithuania), the State Day, is celebrated at Kernavė. During the *Days of Live Archaeology* festival, crafts of prehistoric times and the early Middle Ages, as well as the way of life of the ancient residents of Kernavė are displayed.

Thorough archaeological investigations began in Kernavė as early as 1979, and more than a decade ago the Kernavė Archaeological/Historical Museum-Reservation was established. Unique exhibits are stored in this special complex of archaeological, historical, and natural monuments covering an area of some 200 hectares.

Twenty-eight kilometers west of Vilnius, surrounded by lakes, forests, and hills, lies Trakai, the historical capital of Lithuania. The country's rulers lived on Trakai Island and in Peninsular Castles since the early 15th century. The powerful defense complex of Trakai that protected the western lands of Lithuania from crusaders, was comprised of castles surrounded by settlements and hill-forts. The inner defense system consisted of fortified churches and monasteries, ramparts, swamps and lakes. These often became an insurmountable obstacle to aggressors. In the middle of Galvė, the largest lake of Trakai, stands the gothic Island Castle built in the 14-15th centuries. This is a huge defensive complex that repelled numerous attacks of enemies. In the 15th century it was armed with 15 cannons.

The remnants of the oldest castle of Trakai lie in Old Trakai, some four kilometers west from the present-day town. It was here that Vytautas the Great was born to Duke Kęstutis and priestess Birutė around 1350. Nine wooden sculptures mark the way to his birthplace.

Legend has it that Lake Galvė, surrounding the Island Castle on all sides, does not freeze over until it gets a victim, and that in its depths still lie the treasures of Grand Duke Kęstutis. Over twenty islets of the lake remember the times when life was in full swing in Trakai Castle. Julijona, second wife of Grand Duke Vytautas, used to pray on Bažnytėlė Islet. In Pirtsalis Island, Vytautas would have disobedient noblemen flogged. Those sentenced to die were taken to Valka, while their families wept on Raudinė.

A small Karaite community, the descendants of a Crimean people that came to Trakai in the late 14th century, still lives in Trakai. Vytautas the Great brought four hundred of their families after a successful campaign. The Karaites formed his personal guard, defended the castles, and worked as clerks and interpreters.

Romantic Trakai

Amidst the Lake of Galvė stands a Gothic Castle dating from XIV-XV centuries. It is a unique Middle-Age defence fortification which has resisted more than one attack of the enemy. Nowadays it is a romantic landmark attracting both tourists and locals who want entertainment

Later on, having been granted the Magdeburg rights, they worked as artisans and tradesmen, grew cucumbers and kept inns. To better understand the Karaites, who have retained their religion and customs, one can drop in at a small museum that has an exposition explaining their historical background, way of life and customs. All cafes of Trakai serve the national Karaite dish *kibin* (cakes with chopped meat, similar to a Cornish pasty), and caraway *kvass*.

Today Trakai is a small town, the administration center of a district, with a population of over 6000. The authentic entranceways, courtyards and palace halls of the Island Castle restored more than a decade ago, reveal to the visitors the trials the building once underwent. The exposition arranged in the central hall depicts the most important events in the history of Trakai and the restoration of the Island Castle. On weekends and during the warm season, holidaymakers flock to Trakai squeezed in between two lakes. They are attracted by ancient castles, the unique old quarter, clean lakes adorned with islets and sails of yachts, sandy lakesides... Every August, lovers of ballet and classical music gather in the courtyards of Trakai Castle for the traditional Trakai Festival inspired by the world-famous Russian ballerina Maya Plisteskaya. She has been granted honorary Lithuanian citizenship for her cultural merits. Lake Galvė, with an area of 3.88 square kilometers and the maximum depth of 47 meters, is a venue for international rowing competitions held every year.

The Inner Yard of the Middle-Age castle sinks in a romantic atmosphere reminiscent of more than one century.

Trakai and its environs have been granted the status of a historical national park. It is the only park of its kind in Lithuania and Europe. Over thirty lakes and forests, that still remember the outings and hunting expeditions of rulers of the distant past, stretch out within its boundaries.

A small Karaite community still lives in the northern part of Trakai. Karaites' wooden houses always have three windows facing the street.

Those who want to indulge in the spirit of the battles that once took place here, are welcome to attend a special show in Trakai, i.e. a reproduction of Middle-Age knights' fighting which is one of the entertainments offered outside the Caste.

→ Shrovetide culminates in the Morė being tossed into a bonfire to drive the tiresome winter away.

→→ On St. John's night bonfires make the sky glow all over Lithuania.

Mythology

Christianity that came to Lithuania at the end of the 14th century failed to oust the old religion completely. Its rites blended in with those of the ancient faith, and became national traditions

Lithuanian mythology took shape in pagan times. Customs that have remained until today help to understand the ancient Lithuanians' outlook on the world, their beliefs, and their values.

The ancient Lithuanians believed that spirits, capable of good and evil deeds, lived in nature, spirits full of secrets and surprises.

Pagans used to pray to the sun, the moon, and the elements. They linked natural phenomena with the work of the gods, and worshipped natural objects in the belief that the gods lived in them.

The most ancient Lithuanian deities were feminine. Lithuanians still name their daughters Laima, Dalia, Medeinė, Gabija, Austėja, and Žemyna.

Laima was the goddess who ordained that one be born and live happily. Ragana (Witch) was what Lithuanians called the goddess of death and rebirth. All life sprang from the goddess Žemyna, who also encouraged growth and fruitfulness. Medeinė was the patronness of forests, while Austėja took care of bees and plants. Dievas (God) was the highest deity, the patron of celestial light, day, accord, peace and friendship. Perkūnas, the god of warriors, inspired awe in the ancestors of the Lithuanians. With thunder and lightning he chastised devils, awakened the earth from winter sleep and encouraged it to be fruitful.

In pagan sanctuaries, the priests and sacrificators made offerings to the gods, prophesied the future, conducted burial rites, and saw men off to war. The sacred places where pagans used to pray and sacrifice were called *alkai*. As a rule, these were hillocks and glades on the banks of streams where fires burned on rock pile altars kindled by virgin priestesses.

Christianity that came to Lithuania at the end of the 14th century failed to oust the old religion completely, and its rites blended in with those of the ancient faith. Even today on the eve of Catholic Christmas, Lithuanians sit at a table for a pagan Christmas Eve supper, leaving the leftovers to the ancestors' spirits. On Shrovetide, they toss Morė - a female scarecrow made of straw and dressed in rags - into a bonfire, and thus drive away the tiresome winter. On June 24, the shortest night of the year, there is a lot of merrymaking when celebrating Rasų (St. John's) night. On its eve, herbs having magic powers to cure all diseases are gathered. After sunset, bonfires are lit for the flames to scare away the evil spirits, and at midnight a search begins deep in forests for a fern that blooms for a very short time. Those who are lucky to find one are said to be able to understand the language of birds and animals, to read people's thoughts, and to see hidden treasures.

The Park of Europe

The artists taking care of the Park of Europe, where art and nature blend into one another, want the best modern works by Lithuanian and international sculptors to be represented in this open-air museum

The center of Europe, as estimated in 1989 by scientists of the French National Geographic Institute, is in Lithuania. It is 19 km. north of Vilnius, the Lithuanian capital. Gintaras Karosas, a young artist, decided to perpetuate the center of the Old Continent with the language of art. He created an open-air museum of sculpture in an out-of-the-way neglected forest. The impressive terrain of the park – hillocks, hollows, small ponds – offers a wonderful background for exhibits. International symposiums of sculpture have been held in the Park of Europe since 1993.

The artists taking care of the Park of Europe, where art and nature blend into one another, want the best works by Lithuanian and international sculptors to be represented here. A sculpture erected in 1996 by Dennis Oppenheim, a famous conceptualist, paved the way for other classics of modern sculpture. At present, over 90 pieces of art by artists from 29 countries are exhibited in the park that covers an area of 55 hectares. Such world-famous modern artists as Magdalena Abakanowicz and Sol LeWitt display their works here. Over 60,000 visitors from Lithuania and abroad come to the park every year.

The Guinness World Records agency has recognized the sculpture Gintaras Karosas made of TV sets as the largest of its kind. In response to the request by LNK TV and the Park of Europe, during the event entitled *Give your old TV to Europe* people brought nearly three thousand old sets, many more than the expected few hundred. The sculptor used them to create a maze of TV sets in the shape of a tree with a stem, branches and roots. This sculpture, *LNK Infotree*, is the largest one in the Park of Europe – the maze covers an area of over 3000 square meters. Nevertheless, in support of the author's idea to show the absurdity of the Soviet ideology that was pressed on citizens through 'the boxes' for more than half a century, people are still bringing their old TVs to the park.

The museum of the Park of Europe is believed to be one of the most interesting open-air museums in the world. Visitors are attracted by the opportunity to stay for a while in the center of the European continent, to see the world's largest armchair filled with water, to stand under the world's largest cobweb in the shape of sails, or to swing a boulder weighing several tons...

J. Romualdas Poteskis

J. Vytas Karaciejus

↑ Vytas Karaciejus

Kretinga Conservatory

The conservatory founded in the Kretinga mansion of Count J. Tiškevičius a hundred-odd years ago has become a place where one can see numerous plants that have come to Lithuania from the farthest parts of the globe

There is a place in Lithuania where numerous and various plants from the farthest corners of the earth can be observed. Although smaller than in their native lands, they are true representatives of the tropical forests of Indonesia, India, and Brazil, of African and Mexican deserts.

Kretinga Conservatory is over 100 years old. Count Juozapas Tiškevičius established it in the 19th century in the manor house of Kretinga. Fan palms used to stand in splendor here, banana trees thrived, and climbing plants decorated the walls. Ornamental fish swam in streams winding among the plants. Count Aleksandras Tiškevičius had the Conservatory renovated and new rare species of vegetation planted.

The modern history of the Conservatory began in 1987, when nearly five decades after it had been destroyed in 1940, restoration was completed and the first plants were installed.

A ficus (Ficus benjamina) is the tallest tree of the Kretinga Conservatory, which for over a decade now has been taken care of by the Kretinga Museum. The plant is a typical representative of India's tropical forests. Under natural conditions its trunk could reach 10 meters in thickness surrounded by as many as a thousand or so thinner stems.

The top of the evergreen cypress (Cupressus pyramidalis), a native of Persia and the eastern shores of the Mediterranean Sea, reaches the glass roof of the conservatory. Its neighbor dracaena (Dracena fragrana) is a plant indigenous to tropical Africa and the Black Sea coasts.

Monstera (Monstera deliciosa) thrives in the conservatory. It is a plant of the wet tropical forests of South America. Its roots, 'Tarzan's ropes', hang in the air, and the leaves 'weep' before rain. Next to these grows an agave, a native of Central America, as well as an aloe from South Africa, and cacti, silk-trees and other species. In all there are more than 150 plants imported from different countries.

In early 2001, UNESCO included crosses made by Lithuanian craftsmen in its list of the World's Cultural Heritage.

↑ Ramūnas Virkutis

→ Klaudijus Driskius

Jurgaičiai (or Domantai) mound rises not far from Šiauliai, in the vicinity of Meškuičiai Village. The mound is called the Hill of Crosses. The top of this low, oblong hill and its slopes are studded with large and small crosses. The families of rebels killed during the insurrection of 1831 started erecting them there when tsarist authorities did not allow the graves of the deceased to be adequately honored. Due to the ban imposed by occupational forces, the crosses attained the status of a national symbol as early as the end of the 19th century.

During Soviet times, when the authorities were bent on destroying the Hill of Crosses, they burned these symbols of faith, broke and crushed them with bulldozers. However, new ones appeared as people brought them at night.

After Lithuania regained independence, pilgrims and tourists started thronging to the Hill of Crosses. Every visitor wants to leave at least a tiny rosary or a small cross as a contribution to the hill. Some make a cross of pebbles, or tie one together from herbs or twigs. Now there are 14,000 large crosses and over 40,000 small ones on the hill.

The fame of the Hill of Crosses spread all over the world in 1993, when Pope John Paul II celebrated Mass here. From atop the Hill of Crosses, the Holy Father blessed all people of Lithuania and all of Christian Europe.

A symbol of faith and hope

Traditional Lithuanian crosses combine elements of architecture, sculpture, smithcraft, and occasionally even those of primitive painting. Some patterns, such as herring-bone, zig-zag, rings, arches, ropes or motifs of nature, are associated with the pagan faith, whereas rays, the Eye of Divine Providence, the symbols of Christ's sufferings and the monstrances originate from Christianity. Like elsewhere in the Catholic world, in Lithuania crosses are erected in graveyards and cemeteries to commemorate the dead, as signs of spiritual protection near houses, and to ask God for a favor or out of gratitude. In 2001, UNESCO included crosses and cross-making, one of the most popular forms of Lithuanian folk art, in its list of masterpieces of world heritage.

Most Lithuanian cross-makers are self-taught artists. They have erected thousands of crosses, from extremely simple to intricately carved, all over Lithuania's countryside.

In Aukštaitija crosses are usually decorated with large halos to make them resemble monstrances or the sun, or with small roofs and altars. The Samogitians prefer small shrines and embellished double crosses, whereas the Dzūkai are fond of crosses with instruments of Christ's torture. Of late, alongside traditional crosses different interpretations of old motifs have appeared.

Countryside tourism

Rural tourism is a new branch of the tourist industry in Lithuania. Having formed as late as the mid-1990s, countryside tourism is being developed in an extremely dynamic way. The number of farmsteads intended for recreation has been growing fast, and the hosts are offering their guests more and more quality services and activities. The demand that is growing faster than the supply attests to the immense prospects of this business.

Countryside tourism in Lithuania is not restricted to trips in the country for rest and recreation. Rich and diverse flora and fauna, over a thousand rivers and streams, some 4,000 lakes, forests covering nearly a third of the country's area, and hilly terrain offer wonderful recreation opportunities for taking a break from the hustle and bustle of city life. There's plenty of room for those fond of fishing and hunting, and, in wintertime, for skiing enthusiasts. Those eager to gather berries, mush-

rooms or herbs, or to avail themselves of nature's healing powers are not disappointed, either. National and regional parks, former manors, museums of country life where one can get a glimpse of traditions and customs of the country's different ethnographic regions, or take part in folk festivals, harmonize well with archaeological, historical, architectural, and ethnographic monuments, such as ancient castles and hill-forts, or small towns and villages that have preserved their original character.

According to the data of the Countryside Tourism Association of Lithuania there are nearly 700 farmsteads offering rural tourism facilities in the country. Most of them are small, capable of taking in 10 people or so. A score of Lithuanian farmsteads have been granted the highest category in terms of the services being rendered.

It is probably due to the intense activities of the Countryside Tourism Association that increasingly more Lithuanians prefer taking a vacation in Lithuania rather than dreaming about flying to distant exotic countries for their holidays. The advantage of countryside tourism over package tours is that one can relax in familiar surroundings.

It is impossible to imagine the traditional Lithuanian cuisine without *didžkukuliai, vėdarai, cold borshct*, eggs, and brown bread.

Lithuanian foods and drinks

Lithuanians are hearty eaters fond of good food

Lithuanians are fond of good, delicious and nourishing food. Lithuanian traditional cuisine took several hundred years to evolve. Although cultural links with its neighbors did affect its development, few of the national dishes have been borrowed.

Different eating habits formed in individual ethnic regions of Lithuania, and different foods are favored. Say, the Žemaičiai like *kastinys* (a dish made of beaten cream), kashas, and stews; the Aukštaičiai prefer dishes made of buckwheat, mushrooms, and potatoes; the Suvalkiečiai are fond of smoked meats, *didžkukuliai* (grated potatoes stuffed with meat or curds), and potato sausages; whereas fish dishes are a staple diet of those living on the sea coast.

Since ancient times rye bread has been one of the Lithuanians' staples. It is eaten every day for breakfast, lunch and dinner, therefore, in colloquial Lithuanian and folk songs bread figures as food as a whole. Numerous customs, beliefs, and spells feature bread. It is used for rituals of the Lithuanians' family parties and during agricultural holidays.

Lithuanians also eat a fair amount of meat and meat dishes. Pork has always been and remains a staple in Lithuania. It is eaten boiled or fried, salted or smoked. The Suvalkiečiai and the Aukštaičiai make the most pork dishes. The Žemaičiai also eat quite a lot of it. The Suvalkiečiai give preference to pork fat, and even boil flitch to make the meal "more substantial".

Traditional and ritual Lithuanian drinks are mead and beer. Mead is the oldest and noblest beverage. The Anglo-Saxon traveler, Wolfstan, mentioned mead, a strong liquor fermented from honey that Lithuanians and Prussians consumed as early as the late 9th century. This was confirmed in the 14th century by P. Dusburg in the chronicle of the Prussian land as well as by other travelers and annalists.

In the second half of the 20th century, mead was nearly replaced by vodka. However, when three decades ago the mead factory at Stakliškės started producing this beverage in accordance with ancestors' recipes, mead once again is served at festive meals.

Lithuanians have been brewing and drinking beer for nearly a thousand years. Today it remains the most popular, traditional beverage. Nowadays, beer produced in modern breweries is consumed throughout the country. Only in northern Lithuania traditions of home-made beer made of barley malt are still cherished.

↑ Jonas Kliučius

Banks

The most dramatic
changes in the
country's banking
sector have taken
place over the last
several years. The
largest groups of
banks from
Scandinavian
countries have
solidified their
positions in the
country. The capital
of German, Polish,
and Latvian banks
has entered the
Lithuanian banking
sector

The Lithuanian banking sector is comprised of the Lithuanian Bank, established in 1990 and continuing the traditions of the country's central bank that functioned prior to World War II, and commercial banking institutions operating in the country.

The Bank of Lithuania is implementing the key objectives of the country's monetary policy and is seeking to ensure stable prices. It sets the system of regulating the exchange rate of the litas and announces its official exchange rates, issues currency, grants and cancels licenses to the country's credit institutions, etc.

The first private commercial banks of Lithuania were established in 1989. Currently, there are ten commercial banks licensed to the Bank of Lithuania, branches of three foreign banks, representative offices of three foreign banks, the Central Credit Union of Lithuania, and some 60 credit unions.

Ūkio Bankas, set up in 1989 by representatives of the largest enterprises of Kaunas, is the oldest of the currently functioning commercial banks of Lithuania and the only one with headquarters in Kaunas. Ūkio Bankas, since the first days of its inception, has been striving to meet the requirements of a credit enterprise functioning under new conditions, namely those of financing the country's economy, which started operating under market conditions. It has a well-developed network in all major towns and county centers of Lithuania, and is implementing its mission of contributing to developing businesses not only in major towns but in rural areas, too. The continuously growing and developing Ūkio Bankas occupies a steady position in the market, and is among the top five commercial banks in terms of the assets at its disposal.

The greatest changes in the country's banking sector have taken place over the last several years. Vilniaus Bankas has merged with Hermio Bankas, which resulted in Lithuania's largest private bank. At present, Vilniaus Bankas is being run by Scandinavian investors, the SEB group. The Estonian Hansabank has purchased the Savings Bank of Lithuania and is now the manager.

Norddeutsche Landesbank Girozentrale Bank, Germany, purchased Žemės Ūkio Bank, the last state-owned bank of Lithuania in 2002. It has now become Nord/LB.

Nordea Bank Plc., Finland, Norddeutsche Landesbank Girozentrale, and Vereins und Westbank AG, both German, are among the subsidiaries of foreign banks currently operating in Lithuania. Raiffeisen Bank Polska S. A., Poland, AB „Rietumu" banka, and Akciju Komercbanka „Baltikums", both Latvian, have their representative offices in Lithuania.

↑ Jonas Kliučius

Creating an environment favorable to business

A relatively modern infrastructure has been instrumental in opening Western markets to Lithuanian goods. Well-educated, skilled labor, and a favorable government investment strategy creating a safe environment for business also encourage investment in Lithuania

Lithuania started transforming its state-run economy, the most diversified among the Baltic States, along free market principles as soon as independence was restored. Positive changes became evident shortly after Lithuania signed the Free Trade Agreement in 1995. Trade volumes between Lithuania and the countries of the Old Continent grew considerably.

Products of light industry, electronics, wood and metal processing, chemical and machine-tool industries that traditionally have been strong in Lithuania, as well as agricultural produce, are exported into the markets of the Baltic States and Eastern Europe with some 300 million consumers. A relatively modern infrastructure with four major airports, an ice-free seaport, and a highway network, considered to be the best in the region, has been instrumental in opening Western markets to Lithuanian goods. Lithuania's exports in 2002 were worth over 20.4 billion litas (€ 5.9 billion) and mostly consisted of textiles, machine tools and equipment, timber, vehicle parts, chemicals and minerals.

Foreign investment into different industries of Lithuania has also been continuously growing, resulting in modernization of the chemical, wood-processing, and shipbuilding industries, as well as electronics and telecommunications. Foreign capital has also contributed to upgrading the textile industry, and the dairy and beer brewing sectors.

Well-educated, skilled labor and a favorable government investment strategy creating a safe environment for local and foreign companies to develop business, also encourage investment in Lithuania. The investors respond by allocating funds for developing machine-tool building and furniture production, power economy, light industry, and services. The amount of the ever-growing foreign investments in Lithuania was as high as 13.2 billion litas (€ 3.8 billion) in 2002.

Private commercial banking that has recently grown strong is now attracting foreign investment, too. Commercial banks have dramatically expanded their range of services, including leasing, insurance, asset management, and electronic and investment banking.

Foreign investments in Lithuania give local businessmen a chance to show what they are worth. The headquarters of Kraft Foods, Lithuania, built by AB *Kausta* serves as an example.

Oil refining

Lithuania's oil sector has been operating under market conditions since 1992. In 2002, there were about 290 enterprises holding licenses for trading in oil products and operating approximately 650 gas stations, as well as 4 oil-producing companies, one oil refining and transporting company (AB Mazeikiu Nafta), and one oil product handling terminal (AB Klaipedos Nafta).

Public Company Mazeikiu Nafta comprised of Mazeikiai Refinery, Butinge Terminal and Birzai Pipeline was set up in 1998 as a result of Lithuania's oil sector restructuring.

The main activities of the company include crude oil and other feedstock refining, trade in oil products, loading of oil onto tankers, transporting of oil and oil products by pipelines.

Mazeikiu Nafta produces unleaded gasolines grades 92, 95, 98, and unleaded gasolines grades VENTUS 92, VENTUS 95, and VENTUS 98 with multifunctional additives, summer-grade and winter-grade diesel fuel, VENTUS diesel fuel with multifunctional additives, heavy fuel oil, JET A-1 jet-engine fuel, liquefied gas, road, roofing and construction bitumen, elemental sulfur.

Mazeikiai Refinery, situated approximately 18 km northwest of the town of Mazeikiai, operational since 1980, is some 90 kilometers away from Butinge, Klaipeda, and Ventspils (Latvia) terminals.

The design capacity of the refinery is 15 million tons of oil per year. The implementation of the company modernization program was begun in 2000. After its projects are completed, all the oil products produced by Mazeikiu Nafta will meet EU quality standards, the production efficiency will grow, production costs will be reduced, and the performance flexibility will improve.

The modern oil export/import terminal constructed on the Baltic coast at Butinge was commissioned in 1999. It is comprised of a 91.5-kilometer-long oil pipeline connected with Mazeikiai Refinery, a pump station at the site of Mazeikiai Refinery, tanks in Butinge, an offshore pipeline and a single point mooring (SPM) buoy.

Butinge Terminal can service tankers with a capacity of 150,000 tons. State-of-the-art technologies including a leak detection system are being applied at the terminal. A stringent environment monitoring program is being carried out.

A pipeline with a discharge capacity of 16.2 million tons a year connects Mazeikiai Refinery with the pump station at Birzai located at a branch of the main oil pipeline. Mazeikiu Nafta services some 500 kilometers of the pipeline on Lithuania's territory.

The leak detection system of the main pipelines can pinpoint leaks and promptly respond to a possible unauthorized access to the oil pipeline system operated by the company.

Electricity Industry

Electricity, the most attractive type of energy, is the driving force improving the standards of life and ensuring the progress of economy

Electricity, the most attractive type of energy, is the driving force behind improving the standards of life and ensuring the progress of the economy. In Lithuania electric energy is generated by a nuclear power plant as well as by thermal and hydroelectric power plants. Electricity consumption in the country has been steadily growing. Industrial enterprises consume nearly a third of the electric energy produced in Lithuania.

Lithuania's electricity sector has been restructured in accordance with the trends and the key provisions of energy development of EU Member States, with new, expressly set up companies given the task of electricity generation, transmission, and distribution. The consumers of electricity have been given the right to choose the power producer and supplier. AB *Lietuvos energija*, one of the country's largest and most successfully performing enterprises, following its restructuring, became the operator of the electricity transmission system. It owns several hundred substations, some 6000 kilometers of transmission lines, the Kaunas Hydroelectric Power Plant and the Kruonis Pumped Storage Plant – the main structures that balance domestic electricity generation and consumption.

AB *Lietuvos energija* is maintaining and developing the transmission network. It is also ensuring reliable electricity supply from Lithuania's power plants to distribution companies, coordinating the operation of Lithuania's and the neighboring countries' power systems, ensuring the balance between electricity generation and consumption, organizing trade in electric power, coordinating export and import of electricity as well as the transit of electricity from other power systems via the Lithuanian powergrid. It is a reliable bandmaster of the electric power system that encourages progress and protects the environment.

With a view to ensuring reliability of electricity supply and quality standards, AB *Lietuvos energija* has been introducing state-of-the-art technology and developing its electricity transmission system. Having accomplished one of its principal tasks, that of integrating Lithuania's power system into the electricity markets of Western and Central Europe, and whilst developing regional cooperation, AB *Lietuvos energija* hopes to become the gate of the Baltic States' electricity market to Western Europe.

AB *Lietuvos energija* is continuously coordinating the operation of Lithuania's power stations and electricity transmission networks, and balancing it with the power grids of the neighboring countries.

↑ Jonas Kliučius

Country of origin: Lithuania

Successful modernization of economy and relatively cheap skilled labor allows Lithuanian companies to increase the volumes of exports every year and to successfully compete in the world markets

The Baltic Tiger – this is how Lithuania is dubbed owing to its fast pace of economic growth. In 2001 and 2002, the Gross Domestic Product (GDP) grew by more than 6 percent annually, and by nearly 7 percent in 2003.

Successful modernization of economy and relatively cheap skilled labor allows Lithuanian companies to increase the volume of exports every year and to compete in world markets. Although Mažeikių nafta, the oil-refining company, is still the country's largest exporter, electronic goods, high-quality lasers, fertilizer, telecommunication systems, and biotechnologies from Lithuania also reach the world at large. The names of Achema, Ekranas, Snaigė, Lifosa, Vilniaus Vingis, and Fermentas companies are known not only to a small number of specialists but also to many consumers.

Enterprises engaged in traditional industries such as agriculture, textiles, wood processing and furniture production also contribute to the growing exports.

A good business infrastructure, a modern banking sector, a favorable geographical location have all encouraged well known companies including Coca-Cola, Mars Inc., Kraft Food International, NORD/LB, Telia/Sonera, Siemens, and others to invest in Lithuania.

Domestic financial-industrial groups, say, the SBA and MG Baltic concerns, the Achema group of companies. The *Senukai* Association comprising ten independent trade, service and production companies, and possessing the largest retail network of construction, repair, and household commodities in the Baltic States, has been continuously growing and successfully expanding.

As companies find themselves pressed for room in Lithuania, they more and more often expand their activities into neighboring countries by setting up their branches there and thus facing competitors. VP Market, the largest chain of retailers in foodstuffs and manufactured goods in the Baltic States with 180 supermarkets operational in Lithuania, Latvia, and Estonia, is ready to develop its activities in neighboring Poland, too. Specialists forecast that after Lithuania becomes a EU member as of May 1, 2004, this may become yet another positive stimulus encouraging economic growth.

Anyone who is building or repairing a house or an apartment, or is already settling in a new dwelling, knows that all the roads lead to *Senukai* supermarkets. It is no coincidence that *Senukai* holds 25 percent of Lithuania's market of goods for construction and repairs, and household articles. The retail network originally founded in Kaunas, now covers all of Lithuania. One can find more than 60,000 commodities there supplied by 1300 regular partners from Lithuania and abroad.

I-V 8-21, VI 8-20, VII 9-17

↓ Tomas Reventas

APRANGOS galerija

◄ In sale-rooms of *Apranga* company consumers of all ages and tastes can find something to their liking.

◄ Nearly every Lithuanian knows *Sarma* shops. The network of cosmetics and perfumery shops belonging to this company covers the country's cities and small towns alike.

↑ Jonas Kliučius

↑ Romualdas Požerskis

Roads and road transport

According to historical sources, some 100 Lithuanian roads referred to as tracts were mentioned in reports by crusader scouts written in 1381-1402. The first highways were constructed in Lithuania in the 19th century.

Much attention was given to roads in independent Lithuania, with the 193-kilometer-long Žemaičiai highway connecting Kaunas with Gargždai, and the 170-kilometer-long Aukštaičiai highway between Kaunas and Biržai constructed in 1934-1938 and 1937-1940, respectively.

Sixty-seven bridges and viaducts were constructed on the country's most important 300-odd-kilometer-long Vilnius-Klaipėda motor way built during the Soviet period. The three-level crossroads at Sargėnai in the vicinity of Kaunas is the only one of its kind in the Baltic States.

The total length of roads winding across Lithuania is approximately 70,000 kilometers, including 21,000 kilometers of highways referred to as state roads. Six European main roads cross Lithuania. Motor roads designated with E run across Lithuania from Helsinki to Prague (VIA BALTICA), and from Klaipėda to Alexandroupolis in Greece. The Klaipėda-Vilnius highway has also been recognized as an E road.

In the opinion of foreign experts, Lithuanian roads are nearly on par with those of Western Europe, whereas in terms of density and development of main roads Lithuania is on equal standing as the developed countries of Western Europe. Therefore it is small wonder that 80 percent of all freight is transported along roads in Lithuania, and that Lithuanian road carriers, most of whom have been united by the *Linava*, The Lithuanian National Road Carriers Association, are significantly contributing to the national budget. *Lietuvos keliai* (*Lithuanian Roads*), an independent voluntary association with 24 members, comprises major companies and organizations engaged in construction of roads and streets, bridge construction, research, design and repairs of roads, as well as companies specializing in road works and production of materials for roads.

The country's road engineers are paying particular attention to upgrading traffic conditions and ensuring traffic safety, as well as to road maintenance. Increasingly more safety partitions are being constructed, the pedestrian and bicycle paths are being extended, and the length of lit-up stretches of roads has been growing. To make sure traffic is not interrupted for a single minute, in winter time, when traffic conditions in Lithuania become more complicated, the main roads are monitored and maintained around the clock.

↑ Vytautas Paukštė

Lithuania, a country of transit

Lithuania is the geographical center of Europe, the crossroads where the routes of passengers and cargo traveling from east to west, and from north to south meet. Since time immemorial it has been destined to be a country of transit.

At present, transportation in Lithuania is a priority branch of the economy, one of the fastest developing and most efficiently functioning sectors. The country's system of transport and communications comprises thousands of kilometers of motor roads and railways, including the VIA BALTICA international highway, the international airports of Vilnius, Kaunas, and Palanga, the ice-free seaport of Klaipėda, the satellite-linked system of modern communications, and the enterprises engaged in the transportation sector. The River Nemunas, Lithuania's largest, connecting central Lithuania with the port of Klaipėda and, through it, with internal waterways of Western Europe, forms an integral part of the country's transportation system.

Lithuania, having a well-developed network of motor roads and railways, a seaport, airports, and situated along the Pan-European transport corridor connecting Russia, Belarus, Poland, and Germany, is taking care of further development of the balanced transportation sector in the country. Funds from the EU, the European Bank for Reconstruction and Development, the European Investment Bank, and other institutions are used for restructuring and updating Lithuania's transportation system. The stretch of VIA BALTICA running in Lithuania is also being reconstructed with these funds. The railway station at Kena at the Belarusian border is becoming a modern facility meeting the most advanced requirements. After Lithuania joins the EU, the station will become its eastern frontier post.

The development of the infrastructure of motor roads and railways, of the Klaipėda seaport, of the Vilnius, Kaunas, and Palanga airports, ensuring interaction between different types of transport, as well as the establishment of logistics centers at major transport hubs create favorable conditions for developing domestic and international shipment, including transit, of cargo and passengers as well as trade with many European and Asian countries.

Planes of *Deruluft*, a Soviet-German company, flying along Königsberg–Moscow, Berlin–Moscow, and Königsberg–Petrograd (later Leningrad) routes landed at and took off from Aleksotas Airport in Kaunas beginning as early as the 1920s. In 1937, aircraft by the *Lufthansa* Company, Germany, started landing in Kaunas on the way from Berlin to Helsinki and back. The following year, the Aerial Communication Inspection under the Ministry of Communication of Lithuania ordered two Percival Q6 passenger planes from England. Named after S. Darius and S. Girėnas, the legendary pilots, they would fly to Palanga and Riga during the time of independent Lithuania.

After Lithuania restored independence in 1990, the integration of the country's air transport into the transportation system of Western Europe began. Air routes started connecting the Lithuanian capital, Vilnius, with London, Paris, Stockholm, Amsterdam, and Frankfurt. Kaunas connected with Prague, Budapest, Hamburg, Kristianstad, and other cities of Europe. Today Lithuanian air transport is comprised of four international airports situated in the vicinity of the country's largest cities. Twelve major flight routes cross its airspace that has an area of over 76, 000 square kilometers. More than 80,000 aircraft are provided air traffic service every year.

Specialists of Civil Aviation Administration see to it that air routes above our country are safe. All necessary international flight safety requirements are being implemented in Lithuania. Experts from the International Civil Aviation Organization also think highly of the national flight safety supervision system.

Oro navigacija (Air Navigation), the company responsible for flight control of aircraft, has been providing aerial navigation service in the airspace above Lithuanian territory and part of the Baltic Sea. A reliable system of flight control meeting international standards is capable of controlling much heavier air traffic than there is today. The company also coordinates aircraft rescue operations.

The Vilnius International Airport takes care of over 600,000 passengers a year, although potentially it could take in twice more. It is continuously being reconstructed and modernized.

⏷ Zenonas Nekrošius

Air transport

Scheduled and charter flights of *Lietuvos avialinijos*, the national carrier, take passengers to airports of many countries.

The Vilnius International Airport situated just 7 kilometers, or a fifteen-minute drive away from the center of the city, attends to over 600,000 passengers a year, although potentially it could take in twice more. In addition to the *Lietuvos avialinijos* national airline, the airport services another 12 foreign companies flying passengers to cities of Eastern and Western countries on a regular basis.

The Kaunas International Airport in the vicinity of the international transport junction between Corridors I and IX, hauls two thirds of the transit cargo. The geographical location and technical advantages of Kaunas Airport create excellent conditions for penetrating the intercontinental market of transit freight haulage, as well as for maintaining the leading position in the transit freight market of the Baltic region.

With the growth of Klaipėda's industrial region, the importance of Palanga Airport has been rapidly increasing. The airport handles regular flights to Hamburg, Kristianstad, Oslo, and other cities all year round. In summer time, extra flights are added to Europe's largest airports. From there, one can comfortably reach nearly all major cities of Western Europe and Scandinavia.

Scheduled and charter flights of *Lietuvos avialinijos*, the national carrier, can transport passengers to airports of many countries.

↑ Tomas Vyšniauskas

Railroads

The first railroads were constructed in Lithuania in 1858-61. It was the Daugavpils–Vilnius–Kaunas–Kybartai line that later became part of the Saint Petersburg–Warsaw railroad line. Train service started on a regular basis on April 11, 1861, between Kaunas and Kybartai, also know as Virbalis, a place at the border with former Prussia. On March 15, 1862, railroad traffic began from Saint Petersburg to Vilnius, and from Vilnius to Kybartai, and on December 15, 1862, regular train service to Warsaw commenced, too. The Railroad Administration of Lithuania supervised 943 kilometers of rails. Another 185 kilometers of new, wide-gauge, tracks were laid down over the two decades of independence in the first half of the 20th century.

The first electric trains were put into operation on the Vilnius–Kaunas line in 1975. The Lentvaris–Trakai, and Vilnius–Naujoji Vilnia lines were electrified by 1979.

Railroads today are one of the most important branches of transport in Lithuania. Two trans-European transport corridors run across Lithuania, namely, Corridor I in the North–South direction (Tallinn–Riga–Kaunas–Warsaw) with the IA branch (Šiauliai–Kaliningrad–Gdansk), and branch B of Corridor IX running in the East–West direction (Kiev–Minsk–Vilnius–Kaunas–Klaipėda), as well as branch D of the same corridor (Kaunas–Kaliningrad), along which the bulk of passengers and freight is transported.

The length of operational Lithuanian railroad lines totals 17,753 kilometers. The country's railroad system is connected to the tracks of the Baltic States and the CIS. The line between the Kaliningrad Region and the rest of Russia is the busiest of all the railroads running across Lithuania.

The infrastructure of Corridor IX is being modernized with a view towards increasing the speed of trains up to 160 km/h, and the axle load up to 25 tons. In the Kena–Kybartai stretch of this corridor the train weight is to be increased up to 6,000 tons.

As Lithuania is being integrated into the EU, communication along Corridor I between the Baltic States is becoming extremely important. In the year 2000, an automatic gauge-changing plant was installed at Mockava railroad station, and a through train was launched between Warsaw and Vilnius. Now the passengers no longer need to change trains at the junction of wide-gauge and European gauge lines. The Rail Baltica railroad line of European standard is to be constructed along the Warsaw–Kaunas–Riga–Tallinn route with a logistics center in Kaunas.

The volumes of freight hauled by Lithuanian railroad transport have been growing fast, reaching 36.65 million tons in 2002. AB *Lietuvos geležinkeliai* (*Lithuanian Railroads*) carry the bulk of the freight from the ports of CIS and Klaipėda seaport and back, as well as to the Kaliningrad region. The Klaipėda–Mukran international railroad ferry line, the only one of its kind in the eastern Baltic Sea region, is serviced by *Draugystė* (Friendship) railway station. The ferry is owned by Lisco Baltic Service. A container terminal has recently been commissioned at this station.

Oil and petrochemicals, ferrous metals, chemical and mineral fertilizers, coal, building materials, cement, grain, timber, foodstuffs and perishables form the bulk of the cargo hauled along railroads.

Cargos were shipped via the port of Klaipėda for several centuries. However, the activities of the country's main port intensified greatly when Lithuania recovered the Klaipėda region. In 1923, 652 vessels entered this port, and 667 left from it. As early as 1938, the numbers increased almost 2.5 times. Over almost two decades of the country's independence ships from nearly 50 countries came to the port. In the late 1930s, some 80 percent of Lithuania's exports and 70 percent of imports were handled at the Klaipėda seaport.

During Soviet times, Klaipėda became one of the main ports for exports from the USSR. From there vessels loaded with coal, metals, and petrochemicals would sail to countries of Western Europe, Scandinavia, and Cuba. As recently as some 30 years ago ships sailed from Lithuania to 200 ports on almost every continent.

The Klaipėda State Seaport is the northernmost ice-free port of the Baltic Sea. It is a major international transport center where sea, land, and railway routes going from east to west intersect. The shortest land routes connect the seaport with major industrial regions of Eastern countries. The main shipping lines to the ports of Western Europe, Southeast Asia, and Americas also cross Klaipėda.

Some 7,000 vessels from over 50 countries come to the Klaipėda seaport every year. Ships of PANAMAX type, with a deadweight of 60,000-70,000 tons, and a draught of 12.5 meters will be able to moor at the Klaipėda port after its channel and harbor have been deepened, and the quays reconstructed.

Some 20 major cargo-handling, ship-repair and ship-building companies are operating at the Klaipėda port, and all the services related to marine business and cargo handling and forwarding are being rendered. *Klaipėdos nafta*, Klaipėda Stevedoring Company (KLASCO), Klaipėda Stevedoring Company *Bega*, the ship-repair and ship-building company *Vakarų laivų remontas*, *Klaipėdos Smeltė*, Klaipėdos terminalas Consortium, and others, are among the largest companies operating in Klaipėda.

Klaipėda State Seaport

Klaipėda is also an important passenger port. Passenger/freight ferries ply between it and Germany, Sweden, and Denmark. A terminal for cruise ships was opened in 2003. Special ferries take passengers and cargo from Klaipėda to Neringa across the Curonian Lagoon. This facility connecting the Curonian Spit with inland Lithuania is convenient to residents of the peninsula and visitors alike, and plays an important role in developing the recreation and tourism infrastructure.

Smiltynės perkėla is the country's only company offering ferriage services. Klaipėda seaport whose development is in the hands of the Directorate of the Klaipėda State Seaport, is one of the ports given top priority by the EU, and the only port in the region whose development has been supported by the European Bank for Reconstruction and Development, and the European Investment Bank.

The cargo-handling capacity is expected to grow to 40 million tons annually as a result of modernization of the port's infrastructure and container handling plant, and of further development of a motorway and railway network. Owing to modern navigation management, and marine rescue systems that ensure adequate and safe navigation as well as the safety of passengers and cargo, the port of Klaipėda is becoming convenient and attractive to clients – a leader among the ports of the eastern Baltic.

↑ Tomas Lopata

Higher education

◄ The ensemble of structures of Vilnius University that took three centuries to build, has elements of gothic, Renaissance, baroque, and classical styles. St. John's Church with the belfry, the tallest structure in Old Town, is the crowning glory.

The beginning of higher education in Lithuania is associated with the founding of Vilnius University in 1579, the first one in the Grand Duchy of Lithuania and Eastern Europe. However, Lithuanians had tried to attain higher education earlier than that: the first Lithuanians are known to have graduated Prague University in 1389. Later on, young people from Lithuania went to study in Krakow, Poland.

In the late 15th century, children of Lithuanian noblemen were sent to study at the universities in Rome, Bologna, Wittenberg, and elsewhere. Vilnius Academy (Alma academia et universitas Vilnensis societatis Iesu), established in 1579 by the privilege from King Stephen Batory and the bull from Pope Gregory XIII, at first had only Departments of Theology and Philosophy. Later on, the Law Department was established as well as a library and a printing house. Some 800 young people were studying at the university in the late 16th century, and 11-12 professors were teaching.

At present, Vilnius University is Lithuania's oldest and largest school of higher learning. It has 13 departments, university-type and scientific institutes, a university hospital, study and research centers, an astronomic observatory, a botanical garden, etc. Among lecturers teaching 22,000 students, there are around 200 docents and nearly 1000 PhDs.

Vilnius University is not the only school of higher learning in the country. Many Lithuanian schools started preparing for reforming their curricula of studies as well as their structure and management even before the country regained independence. In 1989, Vytautas Magnus University was restored in Kaunas. Higher schools that in Soviet times were called institutes later gained university status, new educational institutions were set up.

Currently, youths from Lithuania and abroad are studying for higher education diplomas at 31 state higher education establishments (10 universities, 5 academies, and 16 colleges), and 17 non-state institutions (6 of the university type and 11 colleges).

◸ During Bachelor of Business Administration and Management studies at ISM, particular attention is given to students' needs. They are encouraged to master traditions of international business.

↑ Žemonas Nekrošius

> Owing to close cooperation with the Norwegian School of Management BI, ISM graduates have a unique opportunity of receiving western-type diplomas of two internationally recognized institutions, ISM, and BI.

> The ISM building in Kaunas is one of the city's most modern buildings intended for educational purposes. The former tobacco factory reconstructed in accordance with the design by architect A. Kančas has become a modern center of business and education in the community.

> An ISM graduate must be a competent specialist in management, an educated person, and a mature individual. To this end, excellent conditions for studying have been created for the School's undergraduates, masters, and those studying for a doctor's degree.

International School of Management

The International School of Management (ISM) is the first non-state university-type higher school of management. The main founder of ISM is the Norwegian School of Management (BI) with enormous international experience. It is the largest business school in Norway and one of Europe's most prestigious business schools.

Established in Kaunas in 1999, ISM has a branch in Vilnius, and one can make use of its services all over Lithuania. The students of ISM, after majoring in management and administration sciences, upon graduation are given a bachelor's or master's diplomas. The most talented ones can study for a doctor's degree.

As ISM lays particular emphasis on the quality of studies, it collaborates only with professional lecturers, specialists in their respective fields, from higher schools of Lithuania and abroad. Professors from different European countries, the USA, and elsewhere come to lecture on the basis of international cooperation. Close relations with higher schools abroad provide ISM's students an opportunity to take over the experience and knowledge of their lecturers. ISM, always striving for the highest professional standards and quality, develops all its curricula based on Scandinavian experience and high academic teaching standards.

ISM is striving to be a dynamic and modern European school of management. Therefore it bases its activities on scientific research and, being open to the continuous education needs of the society, renders teaching and consultancy services to business companies and organizations.

ISM has gained invaluable experience in conveying modern business ideas to heads and managers of the country's enterprises. The quality of teaching by professional consultants of the highest skills is attested to by the confidence in this educational institution: nearly 20,000 heads and managers from about 5500 Lithuanian companies and organizations have taken part in teaching sessions of different kinds organized from the beginning of ISM's activities.

The establishment of a private institution offering university education in management was an important stage in upgrading the system of higher education in Lithuania. It is a visual proof that in pursuit of the highest academic standards the school is capable of opening up for international experience. Today the combination of international experience accumulated at BI and the professional standards of ISM's faculty ensures the position of leadership for Lithuania's first non-state higher school of management.

Information society

Lithuania like other countries believes its future lies with an educated and incessantly learning society in which people's knowledge, competence, ability and willingness to use opportunities provided by state-of-the-art technologies in the most efficient manner gain extreme importance. Over the past several years Lithuania has made considerable progress in many areas of knowledge economy, in particular in upgrading economic and institutional structure, and creating the infrastructure of information technologies. The country is cherishing ambitious yet well-grounded plans of developing a knowledge economy. One of these consists in increasing the productivity of the technology sector from 7 percent of GDP in 2002 up to 25 percent by 2015. Therefore it was no coincidence that the first world IT forum WITFOR whose main objective is to support developing and developed countries in drawing up and implementing information development strategies and projects was held in Vilnius in 2003. Wide use of advanced ITs in public administration, science and education, business and other sectors makes it possible to ensure the development of a knowledge society, e-government and e-democracy, as well as opportunities for spreading and receiving all kinds of information.

Research shows that the number of people using personal computers has been growing fast. More than a fourth of the country's population used PCs as of the beginning of 2003.

Although the number of those using Internet services in Lithuania is considerably lower than in EU Member States, the year 2002 witnessed a two-fold increase. As a result, 22 percent of the population used Internet services in early 2003. However, while developing the knowledge society the problem remains of creating conditions for learning and gaining experience in computer literacy, and for use of high technologies. Other problems are those of people availing themselves of information resources and the Internet, as well as improving the supply of computer hardware to schools providing general education. Work places and educational institutions still remain the places where most people use the Internet. Therefore public centers of access to the Internet are being set up in the country, and future Internet users are being trained.

Considering society's needs, the number studying informatics and similar subjects in higher education establishments has been increased. According to the data by the Ministry of Education and Science, 5000-plus people, or more than 5 percent of all students of Lithuania's higher schools were studying these subjects in 2001-2002. Conventional and remote studies, development of public Internet centers, the diversity of public information means, as well as the possibility of obtaining and spreading information are instrumental in creating a knowledge society in Lithuania.

ISM is actively contributing to the creation of a knowledge society. Students are making use of state-of-the-art technologies from their first academic years not only during lectures but also while studying on their own.

Many valuable exhibits are stored at the Department of Rare Books and Manuscripts of the Lithuanian National Library named after Martynas Mažvydas.

Over 6.9 million items with several million titles of printed matter and other documents have been accumulated at the National Library named after Martynas Mažvydas.

A valuable object that never grows old

Libraries are not only trying to create the most favorable conditions for readers. They also preserve printed and other documents, part of the nation's cultural heritage

Books were the main sources of knowledge for centuries – at first written by hand, later just a few copies printed by manual printing machines… In different centuries, books were banned and burned by authorities, were secretly taken from one country to another by book-smugglers, and were passed from hand to hand.

Today books are not only printed on paper. They are published in computer data media, and some can be read on the Internet. However, the traditional printed book still is and will most probably remain a valuable object that never grows old. Dozens of publishers in Lithuania issue textbooks and dictionaries, popular science literature, novels, and other books catering to the most diverse needs of readers. We purchase some, especially new ones, in bookshops, and we read others in libraries.

The Lithuanian National Library situated in Vilnius next to the Seimas Palace and named after Martynas Mažvydas, the compiler and publisher of the first book in Lithuanian, can be called, without reservation, the country's library of libraries. It was granted the status of the National, i.e., the country's main, library, in 1989. Three years later, it took over the functions of the national press archive and state bibliographical accountancy from the House of the Book that had been operating until then.

Over 6.9 million items with some two million titles of printed matter and other documents (manuscripts, microfilms, audio, audio-visual, visual and electronic material) have been accumulated at the library. Numerous valuable, old books are stored at the Department of Rare Books and Manuscripts of the Lithuanian National Library. More than 30,000 prints dating back to the 15-18th centuries, and over 70,000 manuscripts and archive documents from the 15-20th centuries can be found here. Preserving printed and other documents of Lithuania as part of the nation's cultural heritage is one of the key tasks of the National Library. Documents are continuously being preserved, restored and microfilmed at the library. Optimum conditions for preserving valuable documents have been created in the new modern depository equipped in the library's annex that opened its doors in 2003, to celebrate the State Day and the 750th jubilee of Mindaugas's coronation.

An important mission of any library is to create the most favorable conditions for the reader. Without any restrictions, Lithuanian and foreign citizens can use the National Martynas Mažvydas Library and its numerous reading halls. Herein are publications from the universal (newspapers, magazines, reference publications, and Palanga summer), those pertaining to individual branches of science (sociology, humanities, law and politics, library science), and those that are specialized (Lithuanian philology, rare books and manuscripts, art, music, and children's literature).

The National Library is preparing and publishing the current and retrospective national bibliography, carrying out the statistical accountancy of documents published in Lithuania, and issuing them with international standard numbers (ISSN, ISBN, and ISMN). The library is central to implementing the Lithuanian System of Integrated Library Information (LIBIS) that makes it possible to make use of common data bases, to automate the conventional processes of libraries' activities, as well as to prepare and issue different publications. To date, LIBIS has been introduced in some 50 libraries of Lithuania.

The National Martynas Mažvydas Library is participating in numerous international projects. It can boast significant achievements in library standardization, bibliographic accountancy, development and introduction of computer technologies, and other areas. In response to the ever-growing needs of the developing information society and the challenges of informing the consumer, it is continuously upgrading the system of information supply services, improving its research, methodological and publication activities, and arranging more than 200 exhibitions for its readers every year.

Books that a few centuries ago were printed in just several copies, enjoy huge editions today and reach the farthest corners of the globe. Publications of many countries also travel to Lithuania.

Over 20,000 titles can be found in the *Baltų lankų* bookshop, probably Lithuania's largest and most modern, in the Akropolis Supermarket and Entertainment Center in Vilnius. Numerous publications from Lithuania and abroad, books written in or translated into Lithuanian, children's literature, an enormous collection of academic publications in Lithuanian, English, Russian, French, German, and other languages, cram its shelves. The two-storied bookshop occupying an area of 500 square meters has turned a new page in Lithuania's book trade market.

The *Baltų lankų* bookshop founded in the Akropolis Supermarket and Entertainment Center in Vilnius is probably Lithuania's largest and most modern.

News agencies

reedom of speech and information is an integral part of
Lithuania like in any other free and democratic society.
The present-day media of Lithuania comprise news agencies,
several dailies circulating throughout the country, several TV
and radio stations broadcasting for all Lithuania, several
dozen regional TV and radio facilities, dailies and weeklies,
as well as a number of specialized newspapers and magazines
that satisfy the needs of the most fastidious reader.

ELTA, the news agency with the greatest experience, was
founded in the provisional capital, Kaunas, in 1920. Since the
very first days of its existence, the agency has been closely col-
laborating with the best-known foreign counterparts. Today it is
an independent national news agency preparing and circulating
precise, reliable and objective information on important political, business, cultural, sports, and other events in Lithuania
and the world. ELTA sends and receives around the clock news
to and from Reuters, ITAR-TASS, DPA, Xinhua, BELTA,
LETA, and PAP.

Every day ELTA receives around 5000 items of news from
enterprises, institutions, organizations, agencies and other
sources in Lithuania and abroad. These are reviewed, after
which over 300 items of news on Lithuania's and foreign politics, economy, law, culture, sports and other most important
events are selected and submitted to users in Lithuanian, English, and Russian.

Government and Seimas (Parliament) members, businessmen, leaders of parties and youth organizations, medics and
athletes arrange press conferences in the modern conference
hall of ELTA.

BALTIC NEWS SERVICE (BNS) having started its activity
in 1990, is the largest independent news agency in the Baltic
States. It releases information on politics, economy, finance,
and other fields from the Baltic countries. The main bureaus of
the agency are based in Vilnius, Riga, and Tallinn. Its corre-
spondents are working in all major cities of Lithuania, Latvia,
and Estonia, as well as in Warsaw, Moscow, and Kaliningrad.

The media

The country's dailies, *Lietuvos rytas*, *Respublika*, *Lietuvos žinios*, *Verslo žinios*, provide comprehensive information to Lithuanian and foreign readers. Some regional dailies, such as *Kauno diena*, *Vakarų ekspresas*, and *Panevėžio rytas* are almost as popular. Specialized publications, like the international magazine JURA/MOPE/SEA that writes in Lithuanian, Russian, and English on sea and transport-related topics and has earned specialists' recognition in Lithuania and abroad, and *Aviacijos pasaulis* and *Lietuvos sparnai* intended for professional aviators and amateurs, have an audience of their own.

June 12, 1926, when Kaunas (Žaliakalnis) Radio Station went on the air, is considered to be the birthday of Lithuanian radio. In late 1927, a radio station started broadcasting from Žvėrynas in Vilnius, too. Residents of Lithuania saw the first TV broadcast from the Vilnius Radio and Television Station on April 30, 1957. Soon afterwards audiences not only in the capital but also throughout the country were able to watch TV programs. Now the national broadcaster, Lithuanian Radio and TV, has two radio and two TV programs heard and seen throughout the country.

Private radio and TV stations appeared after Lithuania regained independence. The first commercial radio station, M-1, first went on the air in 1990.

In 2001, the first digital radio (T-DAB) started broadcasting from Vilnius. At present, four country-wide TV and 10 radio programs are being broadcast; forty local TV and radio stations are in operation.

The Media Support Foundation has been set up in the country with a view to creating favorable conditions for propagating culture and education in the media and to implementing in the optimal manner the universally recognized principles of freedom of the press and speech. The Foundation offers financial support through public tenders to producers of non-commercial, i.e. cultural and educational, information. Several self-regulating institutions of the media are functioning in the country, including the Radio and Television Commission of Lithuania, and the Inspection on Journalists Ethics. The Union of Journalists of Lithuania is an independent, non-political, public, professional organization uniting the country's professional journalists.

↑ Albinas Slavinskas

Vilnius TV Tower

The Vilnius TV tower, 326.5 meters high, was completed in 1980. The transmitters installed inside made it possible to increase the number of programs being broadcast, and to improve the quality of image and sound. Today *the Lietuvos radijo ir televizijos centras* company (LRTC, The Radio and TV Center of Lithuania), that officially began its activity in 1945 when the restored radio station in Viršuliškės, Vilnius started operating, is an exclusive broadcaster with a developed infrastructure of relay towers. The Vilnius TV Tower transmits 7 television and 14 radio programs. While expanding its network of radio and TV capabilities, LRTC has recently started broadcasting digital radio (T-DAB). *Erdvės* (Spaces), wireless Internet and data transmission services, are being rendered with state-of-the-art technology.

The Vilnius TV Tower that locals and visitors have grown fond of, is increasingly becoming a key element to different festive occasions. An impressive national tricolor flag over 1200 square meters in size, flew from the tower's flagstaff for the first time on July 6, 2000, the Coronation Day of Mindaugas, the King of Lithuania, which is now State Day. Every year the country's tallest structure becomes its tallest Christmas tree, too. The garlands of fairy lights first started glowing on December 25, 1999, at the turn of a new millennium. The *Millennium light* project was implemented by LRTC, jointly with the Vilnius Archdiocese, the Oreivystės centras (Aeronautics Center) public company, and the Vilnius Municipality. The Christmas tree consists of more than 5000 light bulbs, and is topped by a powerful beacon. Looming at more than 300 meters, it symbolizes the star of Christmas.

Those wishing to admire Vilnius also come to the TV tower. In fine weather one can see the entire capital and its environs within a 50-kilometer radius from the Paukščių takas (Milky Way) café and the observation platform erected in the uppermost ring of the tower. It takes just 40 seconds to get there by express elevator.

↑ Klaudijus Driskius

TLithuanian balloonists have been taking part in international hot-air balloon competitions for 15 years now and have achieved good results. Hot-air balloon competitions have become the largest and most impressive events of international sports in our country. The European Championship of Hot-air Balloons that was held in Vilnius and its environs in August 2003, was successful to Lithuanian representatives too.

Ballooning

Ballooning, having become a way of life to many, and the aim of life to sportsmen, is becoming more and more popular in Lithuania and the entire world. Lithuanian balloonists have been participating in international hot-air balloon competitions for 15 years. They achieve good results and make the name of Lithuania widely known. Therefore, the decision was made at the 2001 conference of the Ballooning Sports Commission of the International Aeronautics Federation (FAI/CIA) in Berne, Switzerland, to entrust Lithuania with organizing one of the largest international hot-air balloon competitions.

Theater

For many decades Lithuania has been marked on the maps of Europe's theater fans as a country having first-rate theater. The professional theater of Lithuania that has been in existence for only a little more than a hundred years has managed to produce highly skilled directors and actors, as well as to consolidate positions in the international theater arena. Modern Lithuanian directors, such as Eimuntas Nekrošius, Jonas Vaitkus, Rimas Tuminas, Oskaras Koršunovas, Gintaras Varnas and their plays are welcome guests at prestigious international theater festivals, where they are often given the most honorable awards. Their names are mentioned alongside the world-famous masters of the stage and the most promising representatives of new generation directors.

The exceptional features of Lithuanian theater are original interpretation, directors' strong vision, unexpected imagery, distinctive variations on the most recent theater trends, continuous search for a new theater language, and excellent performance of actors.

Spectators are fascinated by the expressive and memorable acting of Vladas Bagdonas, Valentinas Masalskis, Arūnas Sakalauskas, Eglė Mikulionytė, Kostas Smoriginas, Vytautas Paukštė, Viktoras Šinkariukas, Vytautas Rumšas, Dainius Kazlauskas, Rolandas Kazlas, Nelė Savičenko, to name just a few. These actors, having received good training, are capable of acting equally well in plays of different genres staged by directors of different generations. The theater infrastructure that formed in Lithuania since the years of independence allows spectators to experience the dynamic diversity of generations, and the various schools of dramatic composition, direction, and acting. Such plays as *Othello* and *The Beginning* reveal to audiences the diverse possibilities of theatrical art. *K Donelaitis's Seasons* (directed by E. Nekrošius), *The Inspector* (directed by R. Tuminas), *The Sea-Gull* (directed by R. Vaitkus), *The Master and Margarita*, *Oedipus the King* (directed by O. Koršunovas), *Heda Gabler* and *The Distant Country* (directed by R. Varnas), and *The Kid* (directed by M. Ivaškevičius), prove the point. The original and convincing language of metaphors created during the years of Soviet occupation has changed, however, classical and modern plays today are interpreted no less convincingly.

Spectators are always looking forward to new works by such young playwrights as M. Ivaškevičius, S. Parulskis, R. Šerelytė, and H. Kunčius. Owing to the colorful personalities of the directors, the playwrights and the actors, both spectators and professionals recognize the high standard of Lithuania's theater.

➤ V. Urmonavičiūtė-Urmana, opera singer, has become a rare guest in her native land. The world's most prestigious theaters invite her to perform on their stages.

➤ G.Rinkevičius and the Lithuanian State Symphony Orchestra he is conducting are making the name of Lithuania known worldwide.

From classical music to jazz

Professional Lithuanian music was introduced in the early 20th century when the first Lithuanian composers and performers such as Mikalojus Konstantinas Čiurlionis, Juozas Naujalis, Juozas Gruodis, Mikas and Kipras Petrauskas, Česlovas Sasnauskas, and Stasys Šimkus graduated from music schools abroad.

Lithuania today boasts a number of companies: the Lithuanian Chamber Orchestra (conductor Saulius Sondeckis), one of the best of its kind in the world; the National Symphony Orchestra (conductor Juozas Domarkas), the Kaunas Choir (conductor Petras Bingelis), the State Vilnius and M. K. Čiurlionis Quartets, and the *Musica Humana* Chamber Ensemble (conductor Algirdas Vizgirda). The Lithuanian State Symphony Orchestra, conducted by Gintaras Rinkevičius, as well as other companies and performers, are also making the name of Lithuania known all over the world.

The beginning of the Lithuanian opera goes back to November 6, 1906, when *Birutė*, composed by Mikas Petrauskas (the libretto by Gabrielius Landsbergis-Žemkalnis), was staged in the hall of the present day National Philharmonic Society. Later on, the traditions of the Lithuanian opera were taken over by the Opera *Vaidykla* (Performance House).

Established in 1920, the Performance House eventually became the Lithuanian National Opera and Ballet Theater. The mastery of its soloists today is comparable to that of performers of Sydney's and Vienna's operas. The troupes of the LNOBT frequently perform in the world's most famous venues; the most gifted soloists attend advanced studies at such opera houses as *La Scala* in Milan.

December 4, 1925, marks the staging of the first ballet in Lithuania, *Copelia* by L. Delibes. For a long time, Lithuania's ballet leaned heavily on the traditions of Russian classical ballet. A good decade ago it started demonstrating original Lithuanian dance, and the performances by the country's best dancers have earned them recognition worldwide.

The intensity of musical life in Lithuania is attested to by its numerous music festivals: the Vilnius Festival, the Trakai, Pažaislis, Thomas Mann, St. Cristopher's summer festivals, the *Gaida* Festival of Contemporary Music, the *Jauna Muzika* (Young Music) Festival of Electronic Music, Musical August at the Seaside Festival of Opera and Symphonic Music, etc.

Lithuanians became fond of jazz as early as the first half of the 20th century. However, Lithuanian jazz artists received in-

 The legendary musical *The Devil's Bride* written by V. Ganelin 30 years ago but first performed live in 2003, became one of the most outstanding events in the country's musical life that year.

Jazz festivals are one of the country's immortal musical traditions.

ternational acclaim only in the 1960s, when the Vyacheslav Ganelin's Trio started playing. The activity of the group in which another two outstanding musicians played, Vladimir Tarasov and Vladimir Chekasin, initiated a trend in music referred to as 'The Vilnius School of Jazz'. Petras Vyšniauskas, Vytautas Labutis, Skirmantas Sasnauskas, and others cherish its traditions. The pianist, Oleg Molokoyedov, has also created a style of his own. Thanks to these musicians, Lithuania has become known as a country of jazz. New, brilliant performers appear in the country every year, such as Leonid Shinkarenka, Dainius Pulauskas, Neda, Juozas Milašius, Liudas Mockūnas, Danielius Praspaliauskis, Linas Būda, Jan Maksimovich, etc.

Vilnius Jazz, Kaunas Jazz, and Klaipėda Jazz festivals invite fans every year. The Birštonas Jazz Festival that was first arranged as early as 1980 takes place every other year. Several years ago, the annual Vilnius Mama Jazz, the Panevėžys Vocal Jazz Festival, and others complemented the list of jazz festivals.

Mikalojus Konstantinas Čiurlionis (1875-1911) is a unique figure. Although the artist shone very briefly in Lithuania's cultural life, he left behind an invaluable artistic heritage of over 300 musical compositions and more than 200 paintings and prints. Part of them are scattered around the world, some are lost or have disappeared during the wars. All that remains has been laboriously gathered by museologist and art historian, Petras Galaunė, and is now stored at the National M. K. Čiurlionis Museum in Kaunas. An exposition dedicated to M. K. Čiurlionis has also been arranged in Druskininkai, the artist's native town. Born to a family of an organist, the artist was raised in the environs of Druskininkai, which lie hidden in picturesque forests. At the age of five, M. K. Čiurlionis started playing music by ear, and two years later, he could already read music. When he was fourteen, M. K. Čiurlionis studied at the orchestra school of Mykolas Oginskis, one of the greatest lovers and patrons of music of that time, in Plungė. It was here that he wrote his first composition. During his spare time, he drew. Later, he went on to study piano, composition and music theory at the Warsaw Conservatory. Čiurlionis used to spend his holidays in Druskininkai where he took great interest in Lithuanian folklore. He was the first professional Lithuanian composer to start collecting and harmonizing folk songs.

M. K. Čiurlionis

M. K. Čiurlionis' works are overflowing with metaphors and symbols mostly derived from the artist's world outlook and Lithuanian folk art. The picture *The Castle Fairy Tale*.

The Fairy Tale of Kings, a painting by M. K. Čiurlionis, is well known to and held dear by every Lithuanian. It depicts two giants admiring a small village, a symbol of Lithuania, that they are holding in the palms of their hands.

While studying at the Leipzig Conservatory, M. K. Čiurlionis delved into the works of the most famous composers. However, while striving to express his feelings, he devoted ever more of his time to painting.

The 1907-9 period was his most prodigious. His mature cycles, *The Creation of the World*, *The Signs of the Zodiac*, *Winter*, the pictures called *sonatas*, and the large canvas *Rex* were created then. These works are overflowing with metaphors and symbols mostly derived from the artist's Lithuanian world outlook and from Lithuanian folk art. The beginnings of modernism, a style that began permeating the art world in the early 20th century, are also evident in Čiurlionis's works.

In the year 2000, which marked M. K. Čiurlionis's 125th birthday, the world was introduced to Lithuania's most prominent artist. Jubilee events were held in the USA, Russia, Poland, and Ukraine. His pictures were displayed in international shows in Canada, Spain, Italy, and France. In the Orsay Museum in Paris, an exhibition of M. K. Čiurlionis's works, nearly a hundred paintings and prints, was arranged. Presidents of Lithuania and France, Valdas Adamkus and Jacques Chirac, took charge of arranging and securing this exhibition.

Simultaneously with the exhibition, M. K. Čiurlionis's music was played by the M. K. Čiurlionis Quartet, pianists Jean Dube, Petras Geniušas, and Vytautas Landsbergis. The latter has been studying the musical heritage of M. K. Čiurlionis for many years.

Only during the Song Festival can one see so many Lithuanians dressed in national costumes.

The concerts of Dance Day at Žalgirio Stadium abound in impressive sights. These theatrical events are created by Lithuania's best choreographers, composers, and artists.

Song Festival

Song festivals are one of the country's few traditions that continued during the Soviet times as well. Since Lithuania regained its independence, these festivals have brought together Lithuanians scattered throughout the world who cherish folk music and culture

Once every four years, in early July, a song festival occurs in Lithuania. The tradition was born in Kaunas in 1924. The event was very modest, with only choirs participating. The former President of the Republic of Lithuania, Aleksandras Stulginskis, sponsored the first song festival out of respect for Lithuanian folk culture.

Song festivals are one of the country's few traditions that continued during the Soviet times as well.

After Lithuania regained independence, song festivals united all Lithuanians scattered worldwide who cherished folk music and culture. Increasingly more Lithuanians from around the world participated alongside local performers in the events of the World Lithuanian Song Festival. In 1990, when the first song festival took place since Lithuania regained independence, during which Folklore Day was introduced for the first time in the history of song festivals, some 100 Lithuanians from abroad took part. In 2003, there were approximately one thousand among the more than 36,000 participants.

The program of the festival traditionally includes a parade of participants, folk art exhibitions, competitions of choirs, etc. The key events are held in the most popular recreation venues of Vilnius. Folklore Day is arranged in Sereikiškių Park, dancers perform in Žalgiris Stadium, Ensemble Night takes place in Kalnų Park, and Song Day in Vingio Park.

On Folklore Day, all of Lithuania's ethnographic regions are represented: Žemaitija (Samogitia, Lithuanian Lowlands), Aukštaitija (Highlands), Suvalkija, and Dzūkija. Children's and adults' folklore and ethnographic companies perform in the so-called barn theaters. Spectators are invited to take part in all kinds of competitions, to taste white curd cheese, vėdarai (entrails stuffed with grated potatoes or pearl barley) or buckwheat cake, a specialty of the Dzūkai...

When a choir of about 10,000 voices starts singing on Song Day in Vingio Park, it can be heard as far as the center of the city.

↑ Klaudijus Driskius

→ Participants' parade is one of
the traditions of the Song Festival.

→ Antanas Varanka

→ Ramūnas Vikšelis

↑ Schoolchildren's bands and orchestras
play during the Festival alongside those
composed of experienced performers.

The concerts of Dance Day, whose history goes back to 1937,
are theatrical events created by Lithuania's best choreographers, composers, and artists. The program of Dance Day of the
2003 Song Festival, in which over 300 dance companies took
part, was entitled *The Green Tree of Life*.

The main feature of Song Day is a concert performed by a
composite choir in the open-air stage of Vingis Park. When
some ten thousand voices start singing, they can be heard as far
as the center of the city.

Lithuania's nature

Nature is like home to a Lithuanian, protected at all times, not only as a source of resources but also as something to be revered. Therefore, oak groves, holy woods, valuable animals and birds, rivers, lakes and marshes have been preserved since the dawn of history.

Today, natural and semi-natural ecosystems such as forests, marshes, bodies of water, meadows and sand dunes occupy a third of Lithuania's territory. Reserves, national parks and other protected areas account for 12 per cent. The most natural and valuable biological complexes, rare animal species and plant communities are found here. Nearly a third of the country's area is grown over with forests. The southern and southeastern parts of the country are the woodiest where conifers, pines in particular, grow in the sandy soil. Deciduous forests dominate central Lithuania. Oak groves occupy some 2 per cent of the country's territory. Their areas increase as oak trees are actively being planted and looked after. The most impressive oaks grow near the Kaunas Reservoir, in the Dūkštai oak grove near Vilnius, and in the city of Kaunas proper. The Stelmužė oak that still thrives in the Zarasai district is considered a symbol of oak trees in Lithuania. Its trunk is over 10 meters in circumference. The tree is believed to be about 1500 years old, although some say it is much younger than that.

Cattle and sheep used to graze in forests until quite recently. Nowadays, in addition to timber, its most valuable resource, the forest supplies thousands of tons of mushrooms and berries. Tons of naturally growing herbs are processed at a factory in Švenčionys. Gathering the riches of nature brings considerable income to the residents of the Varėna and Švenčionys Districts, the most abundant in forests.

All major marshes are now protected as part of reserves or national parks. Unique plants grow there, rare birds hatch, and interesting animals live. One can spot cranes and ospreys nesting, as well as wolves roaming along remote edges.

Nearly all rivers and streams of Lithuania belong to the Nemunas basin. The River Nemunas itself, whose source is in Belarus, winds along southern and western Lithuania before descending into the Curonian Lagoon. Every fall salmon swim to spawn from the Baltic Sea into the rivers of the Nemunas basin, especially the Žeimena and its tributaries. The rivers and streams of the northern and eastern part of the country belong to the Daugava River basin.

99 species of fish, including 26 marine, swim in rivers and lakes of Lithuania. Pike, bream, roach, pike-perch and perch are an anglers' staple catch. An endemic subspecies of the lavaret *(Coregonus lavaretus holsatus)* inhabits Lake Plateliai. Noble or broad-fingered crayfish *(Astacus astacus)* can still be caught in lakes. Their populations are threatened by other species of crayfish alien to Lithuania.

Mammals of 70 species, from the wisent (European bison) to a dwarf shrew weighing just 4 grams, live in the country's forests, fields and waters. Thirteen species of bats are protected. The white hare, lynx, otter and other rare animals have been included in the Red Book as endangered. The waters of the Baltic Sea are frequented by three species of seals, a rare porpoise, the bottle-nosed dolphin, and the white whale.

Wild boar, roe-deer, red deer, and elk are numerous in the forests of Lithuania. Some 200 wolves hunt here, and this population is optimum, as it does not face the threat of extinction. As many as several thousand foxes and raccoon dogs are killed by hunters every year. Raccoon dogs wandered into Lithuania four decades ago and have been doing considerable damage to its wildlife.

Some 40,000 beavers live in Lithuania, and 13,000 pairs of white storks hatch their young. The white stork is the national bird of Lithuania. It is always well taken care of, and nests are placed for them near farmsteads. There are approximately 330 bird species in Lithuania. This number is not constant, as new species are often discovered. As the places where birds hatch have been actively protected, cranes are becoming an ordinary sight. The number of black storks and predatory birds has grown, however, the hoopoe and the roller are becoming increasingly rare. The population of wood-grouse, although not numerous, is stable. Some 15,000 species of insects and a large number of other invertebrates have been recorded in Lithuania.

About 1800 plant species grow in Lithuania, nearly half of them in forests. Many species have been spreading considerably, like the mountain arnica *(Arnica montana)* growing in the pine forests of southern Lithuania. The dwarf birch *(Betula nana)*, a tree standing just about half a meter high, the water lobelia *(Lobelia dortmanna)*, and other relics of the post-glacial epoch still grow in marshes. On the Baltic Sea coast and on the Curonian Spit grow plants endemic to sand. Over 4000 species of fungi are found in forests, 600 in meadows, and 200 in sand.

The pristine nature of Lithuania, with its fresh colors and tranquility, is as essential to people as it is to animals.

Selemonas Paltanavičius

↓ Dmitrij Matvejev

Hunting

Hunting has been popular in Lithuania since ancient times. The first hunters, armed with axes and spears, stalked their prey on the site of present-day Lithuania twenty-five hundred years ago. The game they brought home provided food for the community, hides for clothes, and bones for manufacturing tools. Having settled down, they gave up this risky and not always successful enterprise and took up agriculture and cattle breeding instead. Arable lands expanded at the expense of forests. Animals and birds that had lived there started disappearing or changed their habitats. The number of forest animals decreased dramatically with the invention of firearms. The aurochs *(Bos primigenius)*, regarded as a symbol of strength, disappeared altogether, and so did the wild horse, glutton, wisent (European bison), sable and bear.

Lithuania's sovereigns became concerned with conservation of forest resources as early as the 14-15th centuries. Jogaila, the Grand Duke of Lithuania and the King of Poland, was the first to place restrictions on the hunting of the wisent and elk. Later on, regulations were set governing hunting, fishing, forestry, gathering of mushrooms, berries and hops. In the mid-19th century, the first reserves were established.

Extremely serious concern in conservation of natural resources was shown in the early 20th century. Thanks to Prof.

T. Ivanauskas, all kinds of societies of naturalists, hunters and anglers were being set up, and the first count of animals was conducted. In the second half of the 20th century the wisent, red deer and beaver were reintroduced, whereas the fallow deer, spotted deer, mink, moufflon, and muskrat were brought in. Raccoon dogs have come to live on the Lithuanian territory uninvited.

Now the country's forests abound in animals, and the hunters have enough game all year round. In March, the hunting season of woodcocks begins, in May that of wild boars, in June that of roebucks, in July that of wolves, in August that of red deer and ducks, in September that of elk, fallow deer, partridges and pheasants, in October that of red deer does and wild sows, and in November that of gray hares.

Recently, more and more foreigners, from ordinary enthusiasts to royalties, have been coming to Lithuania for hunting. Hundreds of hunters from Germany, Austria, Switzerland, and Denmark more often than not are offered to hunt elk, red deer, wild boars, fallow deer, moufflon, wolves, foxes, martens, beavers, and hares. Hunts are popular for wild ducks and geese, and in spring for woodcocks.

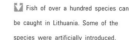

Fish of over a hundred species can be caught in Lithuania. Some of the species were artificially introduced.

Fishing

Anglers in Lithuania must comply with certain rules. The weight of the catch is limited, and sometimes a special permit or license must be obtained for fishing in some bodies of water

Thousands of Lithuanian anglers spend their leisure time on the banks of rivers, shores of lakes or reservoirs all year round. The lakes of the regional parks of Labanoras, Meteliai, and Veisiejai have been famous for their fish resources since ancient times. The best spawning grounds of rare salmon species are protected in the national parks of Aukštaitija and Dzūkija. The endemic lavaret *(Coregonus lavaretus holsatus)*, an extremely rare fish, inhabits Lake Plateliai in Žemaitija National Park. One may catch over a hundred fish species in the rivers and lakes of Lithuania as well as in its coastal waters. Most of the fish inhabited local waters from centuries past, whereas approximately one sixth have been artificially introduced. Current fishing regulations allow an angler to catch and keep one sheatfish, and five pike, zander, trout, grayling and eel per day, and from July to mid-October, up to fifty crayfish. The total weight of the catch is also restricted to 5 kilos. However, the abundance of fish in the waters of Lithuania sometimes produces surprises. Anglers have succeeded in landing a 60-kilo sheatfish, a 19-kilo pike, a grass-carp *(Ctenopharyngodon idella)* weighing 22 kilos, and a carp that weighed in at more than 25 kilos.

In certain places, a special permit or license is mandatory. Permits are required for fishing in the lakes of national or regional parks, and lakes, as well as reservoirs and rivers leased to private individuals or organizations. The administrators of parks, environmental protection agencies and branches of hunters 'and anglers' societies issue such permits.

In Lakes Kretuonas, Biržulis, and Plomėnai, in the Regional Park of the Nemunas Delta, and the ponds of the Verkiai Regional Park, fishing is by permit only. Underwater spear fishing is allowed in Lakes Akmena (Trakai D.), Gavys (Ignalina D.), Kavolis (Alytus D.), Vištytis (Vilkaviškis D.), and Zarasas (Zarasai D.) as well as in the coastal areas of the Baltic Sea.

Ice fishing also has old traditions in Lithuania. Having drilled a hole in the ice of a frozen river or lake, anglers catch pike, roach, perch, and silver bream. In the Curonian Lagoon and the Nemunas near Rusnė, smelt bite well until spring.

Thousands of Lithuanians go fishing in their leisure time.

Summer does not begin simultaneously in the different parts of Lithuania. It takes summer two to three weeks to travel from the southeast areas of the country to the north.

In early summer, the sun continues ascending, and thus the days become longer. On June 22ⁿᵈ, it reaches the highest point in the sky and, after lingering for a couple of days, it starts its gradual descent.

Rain often accompanies the Lithuanian summer. Even on the evening of St. John's Day (June 24ᵗʰ), festive bonfires are often put out by annoying drizzle.

After June comes July with the so-called 'seven sleeping brothers'. This is how the second week of the month is called in Lithuania. This week's weather forecasts the rest of the summer. If the week is sunny, the weather will stay that way until fall. If it is rainy, the rains will continue for another seven weeks.

July is the hottest month. The average diurnal temperature rises to 16-18⁰ C and can sometimes reach over 30⁰ C in the daytime. Anticyclones from the Azores that often visit Lithuania, allow good weather to be enjoyed sometimes for several successive weeks. However, as the sun heats the earth, the moisture it has accumulated is released faster. As a result, cumulus clouds form bringing showers, thunderstorms and gales. Hailstorms can also occur.

The Lithuanian seaside is a favorite place with numerous holidaymakers and those wishing to have a good time on weekends.

Summer

Late July through early August is the best time for taking a vacation at the Lithuanian seacoast. In midsummer, the temperature of the Baltic Sea is the highest during the entire holiday season, and the days are warm and cloudless.

On August 15ᵗʰ, the Assumption, the first fruit of the new harvest and the last blooms of the summer are sprinkled with holy water in the churches of Lithuania. The blooms when dried are believed to protect homes from storms, lightning, fires, and other misfortunes.

While holidaymakers enjoy summer's pleasures at the seaside, approaching fall makes an early appearance in eastern Lithuania. The weather grows gradually cooler, and dew falls at night. A thick fog envelops fields, riversides, lakesides and roads. This is the time when the most beautiful nights of the year present themselves in Lithuania. The sky is clear, the stars shine so bright and so large, they seem about to fall. In August, meteor showers are indeed a common sight.

During the second half of the last month of summer, grain ripens in the fields and fruit matures in the orchards. Storks, geese, and other birds circle over Lithuania for the last time. Screaming cranes form symmetrical, triangular flocks. Although the weather in the daytime is still as warm as in summer, before the break of dawn, first frosts occur, harbingers of fall. The warm Atlantic cyclones are ousted by cooler weather from Iceland, and fall colors replace the summer blossoms.

Active recreation is becoming increasingly popular in Lithuania. In summertime more and more windsurfers are seen in the country's different bodies of water.

↓ Klaudijus Driskus

Fall

Fall comes to Lithuania from the east and lingers for a while only at the seaside. Frosts become more frequent in September, and gossamers glittering with beads of dew drift over the fields. Plants adorn themselves with hues of red and gold. Lithuania's nature becomes astonishingly beautiful.

In late September or early October, the Azores anticyclone returns to Lithuania for a few weeks bringing with it warm, serene and sunny weather. This is Indian Summer. Occasionally it returns to Lithuania as late as the end of October, and at other times, it fails to appear altogether.

September 23rd is the autumnal equinox when day and night become of equal length. People used to think that extraordinary things happened during the equinox. It is believed that Gediminas, the Grand Duke of Lithuania, exhausted after a hunting expedition on this day, saw an iron wolf in his dream, the symbol of Vilnius, the future capital of Lithuania. Therefore, on the last weekend of September residents of Vilnius celebrate Duke Gediminas Day, the birthday of Vilnius and the autumnal equinox. The best folk song and dance companies of the Baltic region come to pay homage to the capital of Lithuania. Colorful carnival processions of children and young people march along the streets. At the end of festivities, a straw billy goat, the symbol of fertility and fruitfulness, is ceremonially burnt. This is a way of thanking the warm season that produced a rich harvest.

During the first days of November when heavy, leaden rain clouds begin to frequently overcast the sky, and the wind strips the trees of their last leaves, when nature is gradually overwhelmed by the quiet of the approaching winter, candles begin to flicker in all of the country's Catholic cemeteries. This is All Saints' Day followed by All Souls' Day when the dead are honored.

On the eve of All Saints' Day, the graves of dead relatives are tidied up and decorated with live flowers. After sunset on November 1st, All Saints' Day, candles are lit on the graves and left ablaze throughout the night. November 2nd, All Souls' Day, is a day of peace and retrospection. Ancestors of modern Lithuanians used to believe that festivities on that day would offend the ghosts of the dead.

Sometimes the earth thoroughly freezes over as early as All Souls' Day, but rains soon thaw it out. It drizzles incessantly throughout November, as a sullen, wet fall arrives in Lithuania. Gloomy clouds obscure the rays of the sun. The temperature drops to 0^0 C. Plants prepare to sleep the winter away, and animals get ready to hibernate. In late November, cool air rushes in from the Arctic regions, and the first snowflakes fall.

↓ Romualdas Požerskis

Winter takes its first steps in Lithuania as early as November. Days grow shorter, the sun shines through the leaden sky less and less often. The weather grows gradually cooler. Sometimes it starts freezing, and the first patches of snow show white.

When the temperature drops to 3-4⁰ C below zero, snow covers the earth increasingly more often. This is a spell preceding winter proper that usually lasts until mid-December in Lithuania. The weather gets colder still around December 21-24, and in early January on the Baltic coast. Now the snow that falls does not melt, and winter sets in. It brings Christmas, the most beautiful holiday of the year.

On the eve of Christmas festivities, December 24th, Lithuanians sit down to Christmas Eve supper. Twelve special dishes are served, including *kūčiukai* (a special kind of biscuits made of flour, eggs and water), poppy seed milk, fish, beans, cranberry *kissel* (jelly-like drink), vegetable salads seasoned with oil, and cakes. Supper at Christmas Eve is a time for serenity and meditation. Traditionally, the leftovers remain on the table because, according to an ancient belief, after everyone has gone to sleep, ghosts come to feast.

In ancient times, Lithuanians believed that on Christmas Eve, on the stroke of midnight, animals started speaking like humans, and water turned into wine for a short while. People told their fortunes, guessed how long they would live and whether they would get married, and forecast if the coming year would be good for crops.

Winter

Changeable December is replaced by calm January. The average 24-hour temperature drops to -5-6⁰ C and -3⁰ C on the coast. Rivers and lakes freeze over with thick ice.

In winter, at least once a month most often in February, blizzards rage that mingle the sky with the earth and cause a lot of damage. After they subside, thaws – spells of damp, fairly warm and cloudy weather – melt snowdrifts. Thaws come to the coast twice as often as to the rest of the country. They are replaced by cold spells and sometimes by severe Arctic frost when the temperature may drop as low as -20-30⁰ C. The earth may get covered with hoarfrost or a crust of ice. Sometimes the layer of ice is so thick that tree branches and electric wires snap under its weight.

A popular horse race is held on frozen Lake Sartai in the Zarasai District on the first February weekend, and nine weeks after Christmas Shrovetide is celebrated with characters that have come from time immemorial. On Shrovetide, the lean Kanapinis always overcomes the fat Lašininis, which signals the end of festivities. The time has come to prepare for Lent, the period of meditation preceding Easter. The cheerful customs of Shrovetide are still very popular. On that day, riotous crowds wearing masks and dressed as devils or all kinds of animals rush into the streets. They go from one yard to the next playing tricks, singing and begging for something to eat, usually pancakes. They carry along Morė – a female scarecrow made of straw and dressed in rags. At the end of festivities, Morė is tossed into a bonfire and the gates are swung open for long-awaited spring.

Spring

As the sun rises higher in the vault of heaven, especially in March, the weather in Lithuania grows warmer. The sun glistening more frequently around the edges of clouds and the snow melting rapidly are the heralds of spring. But the earth does not grow considerably warmer during the day, and nights are still cold. Spring strides from the southwest to the northeast of Lithuania at the rate of approximately 15 kilometers a day. Rivers and lakes overflow, and no snow remains on the sunny side of the street. In March, the hazelnut and alder trees bloom. The first birds migrate back.

People shake off the drowsiness that plagued them in winter. Crowds from all over Lithuania throng to Old Town in Vilnius during the first weekend in March attracted by the racket of Kaziukas (a diminutive of Casimir) Fair.

The history of the fair goes back to the Middle Ages. In the mid-15th century the second son, Casimir, was born to Casimir Jogailaitis, the ruler of the Grand Duchy of Lithuania and the Kingdom of Poland. The prince was a virtuous and pious man whose good deeds earned him people's affection. Having died of consumption at the tender age of twenty-five, he became famous as a miracle-worker, appearing and aiding people in distress. The Catholic Church recognized Casimir's apparitions and in the 16th century he was declared a saint. St. Casimir is considered to be the patron saint of Lithuania, and on March 4th his feast day is celebrated.

On that spring day when the snow just began melting, people would set off to Vilnius to take part in St. Casimir's festival. Peasants would bring along all kinds of wickerwork and wooden goods made during long winter nights: baskets,

 The Kaziukas Fair held in Vilnius on the first weekend of March attracts crowds of people from across Lithuania. Few leave the fair without buying a *verba*.

 It is hard to imagine Easter in Lithuania without originally dyed eggs.

Folk craftsmen sell all kinds of artifacts at Kaziukas Fair.

Jonas Kliučius

Verbas are one of the most striking Easter elements of pagan origin. Colorful *verbas* made of dried flowers and differing in their patterns are popular in the Vilnius region. The tradition of *verbas* reached Lithuania from Central Europe through Poland.

Jonas Kliučius

bowls, spoons, barrels, tubs, ax handles, etc. At Kaziukas Fair, whatever would be necessary for work on the farm in summer time could be bought.

Nowadays Kaziukas Fair is a joyful affair at which earthenware, wickerwork, needlework, and wooden goods made by folk artists, as well as all kinds of delicacies and the famous Lithuanian *verbas* are sold. Formerly, *verbas* were only used for decorating the churches of Vilnius on Palm Sunday preceding Easter. Nowadays they are one of the most popular souvenirs of the Lithuanian capital. *Verbas* in the Vilnius region are made by tying dry herbs and flowers dyed in different colors to thin sticks. The tops of *verbas* are decorated with tufts of hair grass. Recently, *verbas* have become increasingly diverse and sophisticated, preserving at the same time traditional ornaments and combinations of colors. They can deservedly be regarded as unique pieces of folk art.

It is hard to imagine Easter, another spring festival, without originally dyed eggs. As a rule, eggs are boiled in water with dyes, scratched or painted with wax. Before boiling, eggs can be wrapped in onionskins, various grasses or cloth cut in patterns.

At about Easter time, the frozen earth thaws out. The sky is more frequently overcast with cumulus clouds. Trees and bushes bloom awakened by warm rain, and green spring begins. The average diurnal temperature rises to over 5^0 C above zero, although frosts still occur at night and before dawn. Sometimes they nip the blooming grain and fruit trees.

When a dry and cloudless May arrives, the weather finally grows warm. Summer is approaching.

Gambling

Hawaii, the land of the most delicious cocktails, meets the visitor on the second floor of Grand Casino World. In daytime one can catch a tasty lunch at the sandwich bar, and at night enjoy the specialty of the house, a cocktail served in a coconut shell, or some other beverage. Visitors can also try their luck – over 100 slot machines are waiting there.

The third floor gives the impression that the roulette and card tables are hidden in the wild jungles of Asia. Nearly 20 tables ensure that there's enough room for all willing to play. VIP and private colonial style halls are situated here, too.

Officially, there were no casinos in independent Lith-uania for a whole decade. The business of gambling was legalized in the country only in mid-2001, and the first gambling venue was inaugurated half a year later, in February 2002. Since then, the merry-go-round of the world of pastimes set in motion by the passion for gambling, a forbidden fruit until quite recently, started turning at an increasingly brisk pace.

The business taking its first steps in Lithuania is becoming ever more ambitious. Grand Casino World, which opened its doors a short while ago, even before coming to Lithuania set an objective of creating a kind of a small-scale Las Vegas in our country where a good time can be had while engaged in meaningful and diverse pastimes.

It looks as if the objective has been accomplished. Upon entering, a visitor is greeted by an entire world. One can comfortably sit at a roulette or card table, or in a 19th-century-style living room, and enjoy the warmth of the fire blazing in the fireplace and the aristocratic furnishings of an adventurer. In the Hawaii Bar a few steps away, one can have a cocktail, and in the neighboring hall partake of delicious Japanese cuisine. At night, the New Orleans nightclub invites one to immerse in the whirlpool of merrymaking.

Although prior to letting gambling houses enter Lithuania, fears were expressed that the underground business of gambling when made overt would cause numerous problems. So far there has not been a single casino-related scandal in the country, and the culture of gambling has grown considerably.

↑ Jonas Kliučius

⮞ According to connoisseurs, one can meet most local celebrities in the *Galaxy* bar situated in the Forum Palace.

Night life

Night life has not only been intense but also diverse for several years now in Vilnius. The multitude of bars and nightclubs offers freedom of choice for people with varied tastes and preferences. People in this business must be right when they say that it is becoming increasingly harder to find a niche here.

However, the Galaxy Nightclub established at the Forum Palace entertainment center became a fashionable venue as soon as it opened its doors. The connoisseurs of night life in Vilnius maintain that one can run into many famous people of Lithuania here.

The Galaxy… a different world – it was not by chance that this motto was chosen for the club. Due to its impressive premises (a three-story amphitheater hall with balconies, private boxes for VIP club members), and equally impressive video and sound effects as well as the diversity of events held, the club can be considered the leader in its field since its opening day.

However, it would be foolish to rest on one's laurels in Vilnius. One can already choose nightly entertainment in the city not only according to one's taste but also according to one's mood. No matter what you want – to have a good time at a disco, to quietly listen to jazz or just to have a chat with your friends – you certainly have a lot of places to choose from.

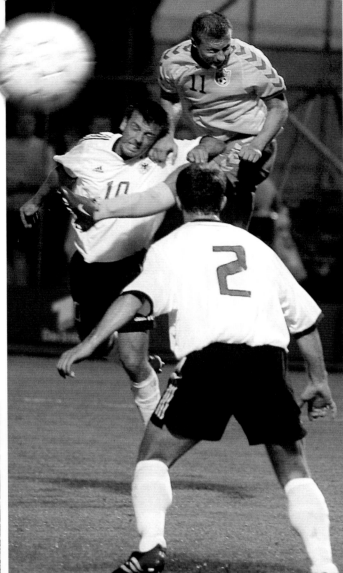

Football

In 1991, after Lithuania regained independence, the Lithuanian Football Federation (LFF) was reinstated as a FIFA (Fedération Internationale de Football Association) member. Since then, Lithuanian football players have taken part in three World Cup qualification tournaments and tried to secure participation in the European championships three times. The national team's most successful performance was in the World Cup qualification tournament of 1998, when with 17 points it was third in its group of six teams, a single point behind Ireland that took second place. Lithuania also participated in the qualification games for the finals of the 2004 European championship. However, to date the national team has not managed to reach the final stages of competition.

The goalless draw in the 1992 home game with the Danes who were then European champions, the draw with Italy, one of the leaders of the world's soccer in 2001, and the 1:1 draw with the Germans, the world's vice-champions, in the away match of 2003, are considered the greatest victories in the football fields.

Visits to Lithuania by FIFA president, Sepp Blatter, the president and secretary general of UEFA (Union of European Football Associations), Lennart Johanson and Gerhard Eigner, and that by the legendary footballer, now the technical director of UEFA, Michel Platini, can rightly be referred to as the greatest achievements outside soccer grounds.

A new stage in football is beginning now that players who have grown up in independent Lithuania are joining men's teams. This is best symbolized by the brilliant performance of young players (born in 1982 and later) in the qualification games of the U-19 European championship, and that of the U-21 team in the matches for a berth in the Olympic Games in Athens.

In 2003, Lithuania was entrusted with the responsibility of arranging a European U-19 championship qualification group tournament for a second time. The first took place in our country in 2001. The Lithuanian side then won against Russia (1:0) and Cyprus (2:0), and in the additional match was just a step away from ousting the British. Fortune smiled on the representatives of the country that invented soccer, and they won on aggregate (1:1 and 1:0).

↑ Antanas Varanka

Increasingly more Lithuanians spend their leisure time in sport clubs. The sport club situated in the Forum Palace offers its clients the widest range of services. One can build a good sweat here, get medical advice, and have a special training program. Entertainment, and learning programs can be arranged. The restaurant offers a special nutritious menu.

M. Drobiazko and P. Vanagas, figure skaters from Lithuania, who have won world-wide fame, have made this branch of sports even more popular throughout the country.

Golf is a relatively new sport in Lithuania. *Elnias* golf club in Didžiosios Lapės near Kaunas is the country's first golf club. Nevertheless the club that has joined the European and World Golf Associations of national federations only a short while ago is already getting ready to participate in the world's amateur tournaments.

Basketball

Both, the country's people and foreigners watching Lithuania from afar, agree that basketball is a second religion to Lithuanians

Some say that Lithuanians, besides being of the Catholic faith, also worship basketball. If there still remains any lingering doubt, the night of September 15, 2003,was a reassurance. After the Lithuanian men's team won the 33rd European championship, the entire country miraculously changed. People who had not taken much interest in basketball before, celebrated the victory in the streets together with hundreds of thousands of fans; irreconcilable enemies congratulated one another, and Gediminas Avenue, the capital's main thoroughfare, was renamed the Basketball Alley of Fame before you could say Jack Robinson.

Lithuanians won the gold of European basketball after a 64-year interval. The Lithuanian men's team first took the highest step on the podium in 1937. Two years later, they became the champions of the Old Continent once again. The Lithuanian women's basketball team also won the gold of the European championship in 1997.

Names of many Lithuanians have been etched in gold in the world history of basketball. When in the final of the 1972 Olympics US basketball players suffered their first defeat in the history of the Olympic Games, M. Paulauskas was captain of the victorious USSR team. When the Soviet team was again awarded the gold at the 1988 Olympics in Seoul, having won against US and Yugoslav teams that were considered to be the favorites to win the tournament, it was A. Sabonis, R. Kurtinaitis, V. Chomičius and Š. Marčiulionis who contributed most to the victory.

After Lithuania regained independence, basketball also made its name known far and wide. During its first appearance at the 1992 Olympic Games in Barcelona, the country's basketball team won the bronze. The team repeated this success in the next two Olympics (in 1996 and 2000). In Sydney, the Lithuanian team was the first to seriously challenge the dominance of the US team composed of NBA stars. The *Dream Team*, having overwhelmingly crushed their opponents one after another, won the game against the Lithuanians by the slenderest of margins.

The men's basketball team of independent Lithuania also boasts the silver of the 1995 European championship. The country's junior team was awarded the gold in the 1994 European, and the silver in the 2003 World championships.

The national men's team that won the gold of the European Basketball Championships after a 64-year interval gave a cause for jubilation not only for themselves, but for hundreds of thousands of people, too.

Žalgiris Kaunas

The history of *Žalgiris* Kaunas basketball club, celebrating its 60th anniversary in 2004, represents an entire epoch in the history of Lithuanian sports. Both, grand victories and dismal defeats are recorded in the club's chronicle. However, *Žalgiris* has always been more than just a team in Lithuania.

The Kaunas club whose name is linked to a historical event important to every Lithuanian during the Soviet period, was a stronghold of Lithuanian spirit. When *Žalgiris* Kaunas and CSKA Moscow entered the basketball court for a win-or-die match, time seemed to stand still for two hours not only in the streets of Kaunas but throughout Lithuania.

Kaunas is the cradle and recognized capital of Lithuanian basketball. It was here that the most sensational victories of the men's national team were won at European championships of 1937 and 1939. It was here that in later years our basketball stars, hailed as masters worldwide, grew up and matured: Stepas Butautas, Vincas Sercevičius, Justinas Lagunavičius, Kazys Petkevičius, Stasys Stonkus, Modestas Paulauskas, Arvydas Sabonis, Rimas Kurtinaitis, Valdemaras Chomičius, Sergejus Jovaiša, Šarūnas Marčiulionis, and Šarūnas Jasikevičius. Most of them staunchly defended the colors of *Žalgiris*. Some players, who began their career with *Žalgiris*, successfully represented the most famous foreign clubs. On the court and in their personal lives they displayed the stereotype of residents of the provisional capital that formed between World War I and II – that of a proud patriots of the homeland, who did their job in a dignified and calm manner. Five titles of the USSR champions at the time when the political imperative demanded that the Soviet army club or at least a Moscow club be the champion, the 1998 victory of the European Cup, the

1999 champions' title of the Euroleague, the 1986 victory in R. W. Jones' Intercontinental Cup tournament – are just the most memorable achievements of the team. Many rich clubs abroad, let alone other Lithuanian teams, cannot boast such victories.

In appreciation of *Žalgiris's* contribution to the development of basketball, international basketball specialists entered the Kaunas club in the list of the world's 25 legendary teams, along with the Boston *Celtics*, the Los Angeles *Lakers*, *Real* Madrid, and other famous clubs.

Arvydas Sabonis undoubtedly is the most prominent star in *Žalgiris* and in the entire constellation of Lithuanian basketball. Under his auspices and with his funds the A. Sabonis Basketball School was founded in 1994 where nearly 700 young players are learning the secrets of basketball, and getting ready to replace the best players of the present-day *Žalgiris* and other teams. A. Sabonis, known as Sabas to many, while thinking about the needs of young players and *Žalgiris*, has recently undertaken a major project – the construction of a new basketball arena meeting European standards. In the summer of 2003, the legend of Lithuanian basketball astounded the whole world of basketball when he rejected a several-million-dollar contract with NBA's Portland *Trail Blazers*, and returned to the team with which he began his career in sports instead. He is willing to help his team return to the path of victory both with his play and his activity outside the court.

There have been ups and downs in the history of *Žalgiris* club. However, as long as basketball remains a force that consolidates our society, and the name of *Žalgiris* means the same to a Lithuanian until today, the basketball stars will inspire hope of new victories.

A. Sabonis School of Basketball trains players for the legendary *Žalgiris*.

The Euroleague Cup won by *Žalgiris* is the most impressive trophy in the history of basketball clubs of independent Lithuania.

The Lithuanian masters of aerobatics, and their leader J. Kairys in particular, are making the country's name famous all over the world.

Sportinė aviacija, aircraft building company, has proven that gliders made in Lithuania are up to the highest standards.

A passion for flying

Lithuania is the only country where children are taught to fly, too. Flying schools have been set up in many towns of Lithuania

The Lithuanians' passion for flying surprises the world. Twenty-three airports are registered in our country, including 4 international and 5 private, the same number of aviation training enterprises, and 66 aviation sport clubs. Nearly 600 airplanes are listed in the register of Lithuania's civil aircraft. Sixteen organizations engaged in technical supervision of aircraft are operating in the country; 8 international airlines and 9 domestic carriers are providing air transportation services.

Aircraft model constructors, pilots of aerobatic planes and air balloons, as well as glider flyers are making the name of Lithuania known at international competitions. Paragliding and hang gliding are sports that have come to Lithuania most recently and have also achieved good results. Lithuania's most famous pilot known the world over is Jurgis Kairys, an ace of aerobatics who won the World Grand Prix of Aerobatics in 2001.

Some 100 aviation events are held in Lithuania annually and increasingly more international competitions are successfully organized here. In 2001, the first World Championship of Gliding for Women was held at Pociūnai. Įstra Airport was the venue for the 13th European Championship of Aerobatics in 2002.

Lithuania also has old traditions of gliding. Having reoriented itself towards Western markets, the Sportinė Aviacija (Sports Aviation) company started producing more advanced gliders that have a competitive edge against foreign-made counterparts and are now being exported to 30 countries. They are known and highly thought of not only in Europe but also in America, Australia, Africa, and the countries of CIS.

Lithuania is the only country where children as young as 10-16 are taught to fly. Gliding hobby groups, clubs and schools attended by several hundred young glider-flyers have been set up in many towns of Lithuania.

The Flying Training Center at Kėdainiai is the only one of its kind in Europe where civilians are also given an opportunity to fly and to learn to pilot L-29 private jets.

The country's first specialized newspaper, *Aviacijos pasaulis* (The World of Aviation), owes its appearance to the Lithuanians' passion for flying. The newspaper's editorial office has already become the country's center of information on aviation.

→ Romualdas Požerskis (118-119)

→ Leonas Jovša

 A replica of *Lituanica* crisscrossed the sky during the celebration commemorating the 70th anniversary of the legendary flight.

They conquered the Atlantic Ocean

The feat of S. Darius and S. Girėnas is still considered a symbol of unwavering love of one's homeland that will be remembered by many generations to come.

At 6:24 A.M. local time on June 15, 1933, the tiny air plane *Lituanica* piloted by Steponas Darius and Stasys Girėnas rolled onto the runway of Floyd Bennett Field airport in New York ready for a flight to Lithuania. With the engine running at full throttle, the nearly overloaded *Lituanica*, swaying from side to side, managed to take off in the last inches of the 1280-meter-long runway.

On the afternoon of July 16, 1933, the Atlantic Ocean was conquered! S. Darius made this entry in the logbook: "Not far from Europe, we encountered a storm." Probably to avoid the storm's center, S. Darius adjusted the route and near Ireland turned the plane over northern Scotland and the North Sea towards the town of Kiel in Germany.

In 37 hours and 11 minutes, the pilots covered a distance of 6411 kilometers but at 00:36 hours Berlin time the flight of *Lituanica* was interrupted in Germany, in the vicinity of Soldin (currently in Poland, the village of Pszczelnik in Mysliborz County). Both pilots perished with only 650 kilometers remaining to Kaunas Airport, their final destination.

The flight by S. Darius and S. Girėnas at that time was the second in the world in terms of the distance covered, and the fourth in terms of the time spent in the air. Although the pilots did not have modern navigational equipment, or any means of radio communication, and the weather conditions were adverse, their flight was one of the most accurate in the world's history of aviation. Before them, 73 attempts had been made to fly across the Atlantic Ocean, but only some 30 had been successful, and only three times had pilots managed to fly more than 6000 kilometers without landing. S. Darius and S. Girėnas were the first to officially take mail from the American continent to Europe by air.

The feat of S. Darius and S. Girėnas is still considered a symbol of unwavering love of one's homeland that will be remembered by many generations to come.

↱ (116-117)
The giant oak-tree of Stelmužė, one of the oldest in Europe, grows in the Zarasai District. The tree standing 23 meters is 3.5 meters thick and has a circumference of 13 meters at ground level. It is believed to be about 1500 years old.